An Assessment of the Investment Climate in Nigeria

Giuseppe Iarossi, Peter Mousley,
and Ismail Radwan

THE WORLD BANK
Washington, DC

1818 H Street NW
Washington DC 20433
Telephone: 202-473-1000
Internet: www.worldbank.org
E-mail: feedback@worldbank.org

ISBN-13: 978-0-8213-7797-0
eISBN-13: 978-0-8213-7811-3
DOI: 10.1596/978-0-8213-7797-0

Cover photo: © World Bank/Curt Carnemark

Library of Congress Cataloging-in-Publication Data

Iarossi, Giuseppe.
   An assessment of the investment climate in Nigeria / Giuseppe Iarossi, Peter Mousley, Ismail Radwan.
      p. cm.
   ISBN 978-0-8213-7797-0 -- ISBN 978-0-8213-7811-3 (electronic)
   1. Investments--Nigeria. I. Mousley, Peter, 1956- II. Radwan, Ismail. III. Title.
HG5881.A3.I27 2009
330.9669--dc22

                                                                    2008051178

Contents

Figures

Tables

Box

Appendix Figures

Appendix Tables

Preface and Acknowledgments

This book is a shorter version of the Nigeria Investment Climate Assessment (ICA) produced in June 2008 by the Finance and Private Sector Development Group of the World Bank's Africa Region and the African Development Bank under the Joint World Bank Group–DFID Nigeria Investment Climate Program. Those interested in more details should read the full ICA report available at www.worldbank.org/afr/aftps.

Although this report was prepared by Giuseppe Iarossi, Peter Mousley, and Ismail Radwan, the full ICA study was produced by a larger team, which also included Elena Bardasi, Ricardo Gonçalves, Sina Grasmann, James Habyarimana, Peter Ondiege, Mohammed Salisu, and Sofia Silva—each having responsibility for different chapters. Numerous other people participated in the completion of the report, and their names are listed in the ICA's acknowledgments section.

The analysis is based on a survey of 2,387 establishments. The design of the survey and the management of the data collection process were led by Giuseppe Iarossi and Giovanni Tanzillo. The data collection field work was conducted by Etude Economique Conseil (EEC Canada) during the September 2007–February 2008 period.

Particular acknowledgments are due to the Federal Ministry of Finance and the DFID Country Office in Nigeria. The former for its leadership in promoting a state-level approach to investment climate analysis; the latter for its sustained commitment and financial support to the Investment Climate Program. Without these champions, this major survey work and report would not have been possible.

Overview

Nigeria's economy has been booming since 2003. Higher oil prices and a series of home-grown economic reforms have put the country firmly on the road to middle-income status. Nigeria's growth strategy, the National Economic Empowerment and Development Strategy (NEEDS), targeted improved public finances and a better economy through structural and institutional reforms. Complementary strategies took the reform impetus to the 36 states. The strategies recognized the importance of the private sector for growth and poverty reduction.

What are the challenges that Nigeria's businesses face today? Since the strategies were developed, a number of improvements have been made but significant challenges still remain. What can government do to promote job creation? What are the roles of the federal and state governments in promoting private sector growth? This Investment Climate Analysis aims to provide answers to these questions. Built on a robust survey of more than 2,300 firms, the analysis provides evidence-based recommendations designed to support the president's seven-point agenda and improve the investment climate in Nigeria.

Government must move quickly to tackle job creation and poverty reduction. With one in five Nigerians unemployed, the country is not maximizing its human resource potential. Demographic trends are equally alarming. Each year, as few as 1 in 10 of the 6 million new entrants to the workforce finds employment. And youth unemployment is estimated at about 60 percent.

For years Nigerian businesses have faced a tough environment. A desperate shortage of energy and a poor transportation network as well as low levels of education and continuing unrest in the Niger Delta have all played a part in a declining manufacturing sector and reduced competitiveness. And yet Nigeria's inventive businessmen and women continue to find ways of coping. The resilience of the private sector promises a much improved performance if government and the private sector can partner to remove some of the largest obstacles to doing business.

Nigeria's workers need to be more productive to compete in a globalized 21st century economy. A Nigerian worker in the manufacturing sector is paid about $200 per month. This is lower than a number of Nigeria's competitors. And yet they produce less than $500 per month (see figure 1). When their output is compared with their cost, Nigeria's workers are shown to be less productive than their counterparts in more dynamic countries such as Kenya, Brazil, and India.

Improving productivity will take simultaneous efforts to foster competition, to improve the business environment as well as to facilitate better management within individual firms. Unlike those in other countries, the

Figure 1   Nigeria—Low Labor Productivity and High Unit Labor Costs

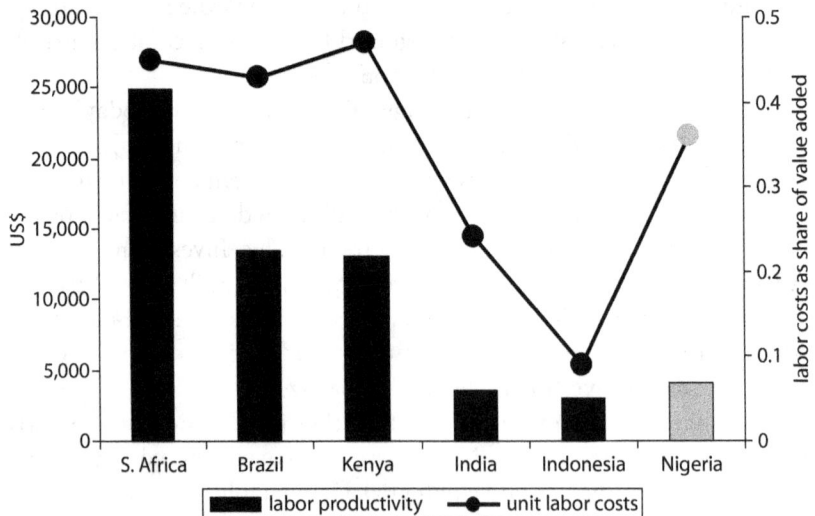

best firms in Nigeria have not been able to grow larger and take a bigger market share. To allow that to happen, policy makers need to identify and eliminate the obstacles to competition by reducing barriers to entry; simplifying taxes, property registration, and licenses; and facilitating trade across borders.

Entrepreneurialism and good management make a difference. Using a new approach to measure managerial capability, the report shows that Nigerian firms that are better managed are 60 percent to 80 percent more productive than firms that are not (see figure 2). A higher level of education and more experience create a better manager. Firms whose managers have a university education are 40 percent more likely to be better managed than those whose managers have little or no education. And firms with better management are more likely to provide skills training to their employees.

Good managers can in part overcome a weak investment climate. Our survey shows that good managers can be almost as productive in a poor business environment as poor managers are in a good environment. The message is clear—building a better business environment is not the only way to improve firm productivity. In the best business environments, firms with better managers achieve 30 percent to 40 percent greater productivity than those with poor managers (see figure 3). Better still, improve both investment climate and enterprise management, as both reap productivity gains.

Figure 2   Value Added per Worker by Managerial Performance

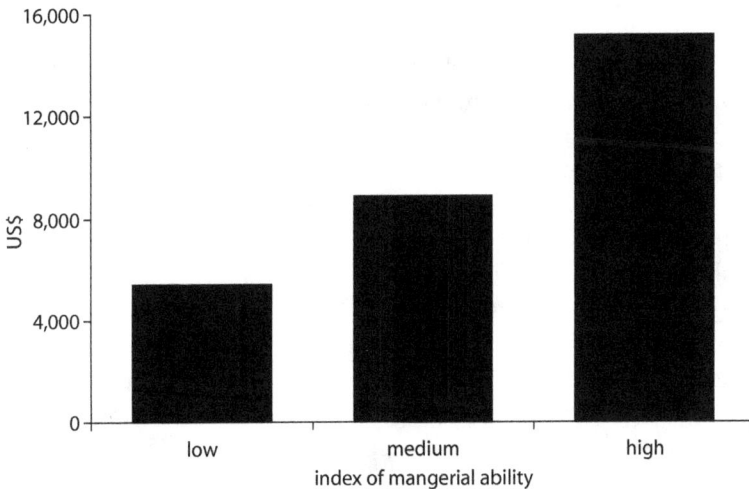

Figure 3   Productivity Differentials Due to Good Management Performance in Strong and Weak State Environments

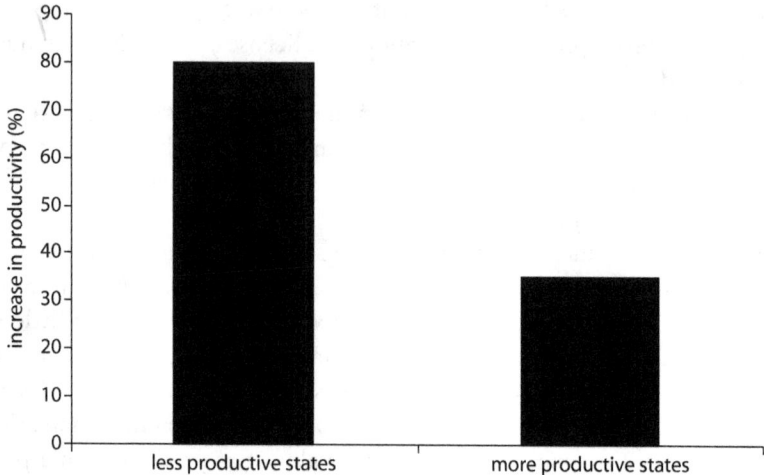

The results of this analysis call for a dual approach in policy intervention. First, in states with a more dynamic business environment, populated by more entrepreneurial firms, attention should focus not on general management improvements, but rather on specific technical inputs supporting key technology or business innovations relevant to specific operations. Second, in the case of environments in which there is weaker entrepreneurship, support to the firms is more likely to be focused on broad-based management practice and financial management training versus targeted technology adaptation and business process training.

In Nigeria the cost of a poor business environment is significant. Our study has shown that investment climate constraints add substantially to the cost of doing business. Each year 16 percent of sales are lost as a result of unreliable power, transport delays, crime, and corruption. And our study shows that in Nigeria, the three most important constraints to doing business are power, access to finance, and transport (see figure 4).

Solving the electricity crisis must remain at the very top of the policy agenda. Electricity is by far the main obstacle. Some 80 percent of firms rank it as the top constraint (see figure 5). Every year almost 10 percent of sales are lost due to power outages. All types of firms, irrespective of size, location, export orientation, and ownership complain about electricity shortages. All firms experience power outages and 85 percent own a generator. This is higher than any of Nigeria's comparator countries.

Figure 4   Indirect Costs as Percentage of Total Sales—International Comparison

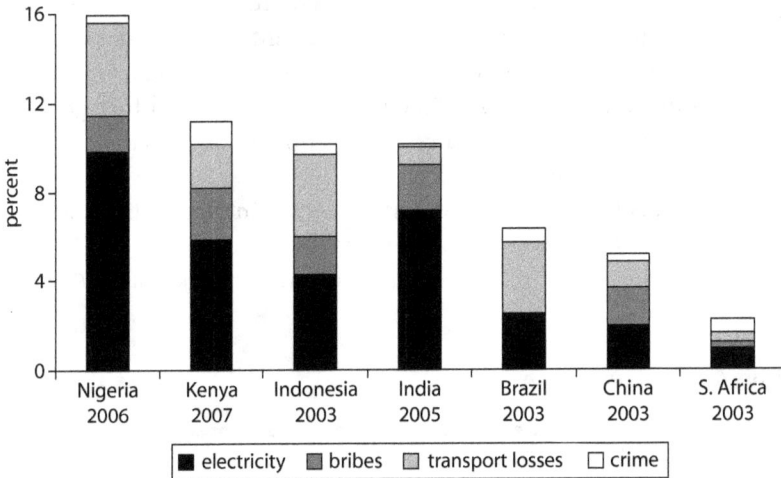

Legend: ■ electricity   ▨ bribes   ▨ transport losses   □ crime

Figure 5   Share of Firms Ranking Electricity as One of the Top Three Constraints

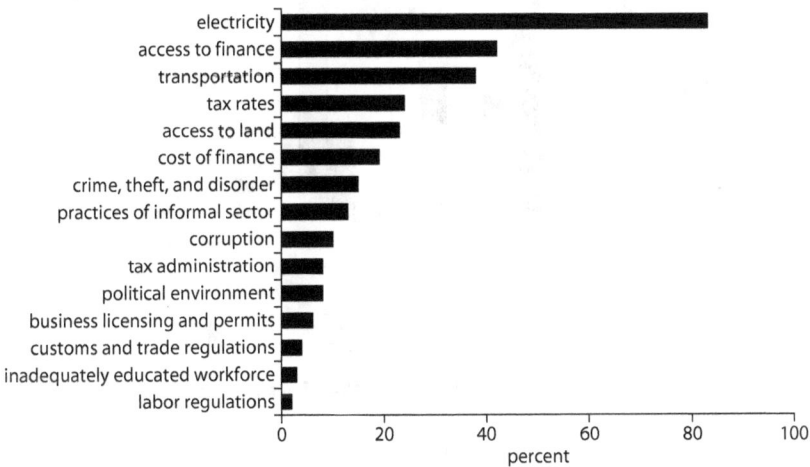

Nigeria's businesses are starved of capital. Although 80 percent of firms would like to have a loan, only 5 percent actually have one. Small firms are particularly affected. Only 20 percent of small firms that did not apply for a loan said that they did not need credit. And when firms in Nigeria do manage to obtain a loan, the time they have to repay it is shorter than that in any of the comparator countries.

As a consequence, **Nigeria's firms have learned to rely almost exclusively on their own funds** for both short-term (70 percent) and long-term

(90 percent) financing (see figure 6). The only other source of finance outside the firm is trade credit, which accounts for just 25 percent of short-term funds. Again in all comparator countries, firms enjoy greater access to bank finance. As in many other countries, smaller firms find access to finance more of a problem than do larger and foreign firms. Smaller firms are put off by a complex application process as well as by the onerous collateral requirements.

Transport is the third most important constraint accounting for 4 percent of annual sales losses. Because more than two-thirds of all Nigerian inputs are delivered by road, the quality of the network is a key issue for

Figure 6   Access to Finance

A: Access to credit—international comparison

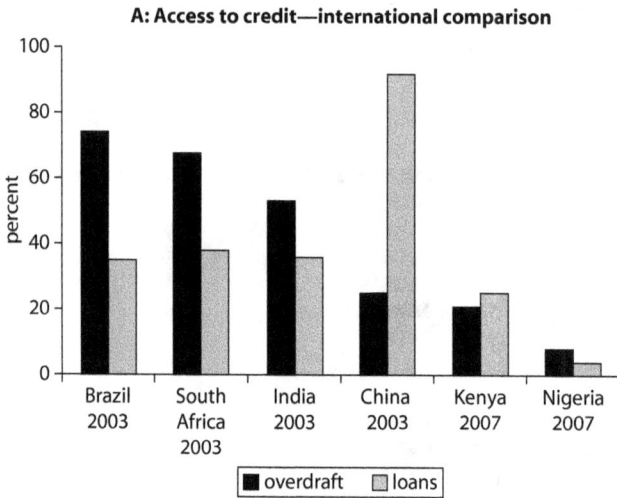

B: Sources of credit for Nigerian businesses

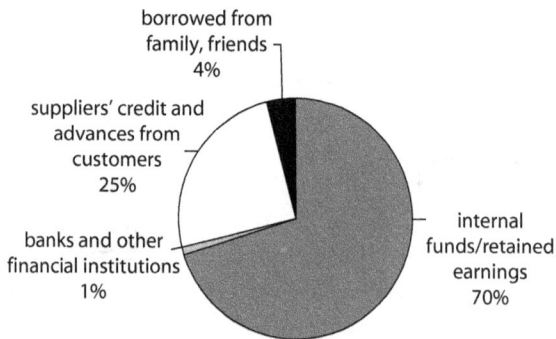

the whole economy. Similarly the efficiency of customs clearances is also a critical factor in transport efficiency. In Nigeria it takes 46 days to clear imports, the second highest among comparator countries. Of all comparator countries, Nigeria remains the most expensive location from which to ship imports or exports—it costs $1,730 or $2,450 to ship a 40-foot container for export or import, respectively (see figure 7).

Different states have vastly different business climates. Finance is a big problem for firms in Abuja, but much less so for firms in Enugu. Similarly, access to land is a problem in Bauchi, but only few firms complain about it in Sokoto. This implies that federal reforms to improve the business climate must be accompanied by state-level reforms to achieve the maximum benefit. It also implies that specific reform programs will differ from state to state.

Our combined index shows Bauchi with the best investment climate and Sokoto with the worst (see figure 8). To compare the 11 states and identify the state with the best business environment in Nigeria, we have constructed a composite index using 44 business environment indicators. According to this ranking, the 11 Nigerian states can be classified into four groups. The first group of states with the best investment climate includes Bauchi and Abuja. They are followed by Kano, Anambra,

Figure 7   Typical Charge for a 40-Foot Export and Import Container

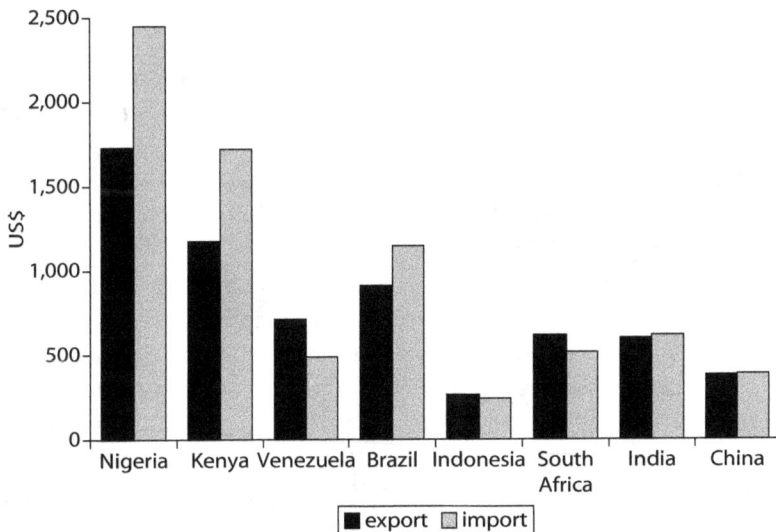

Source: Connecting to compete.

Figure 8   Investment Climate Index in 11 Nigerian States

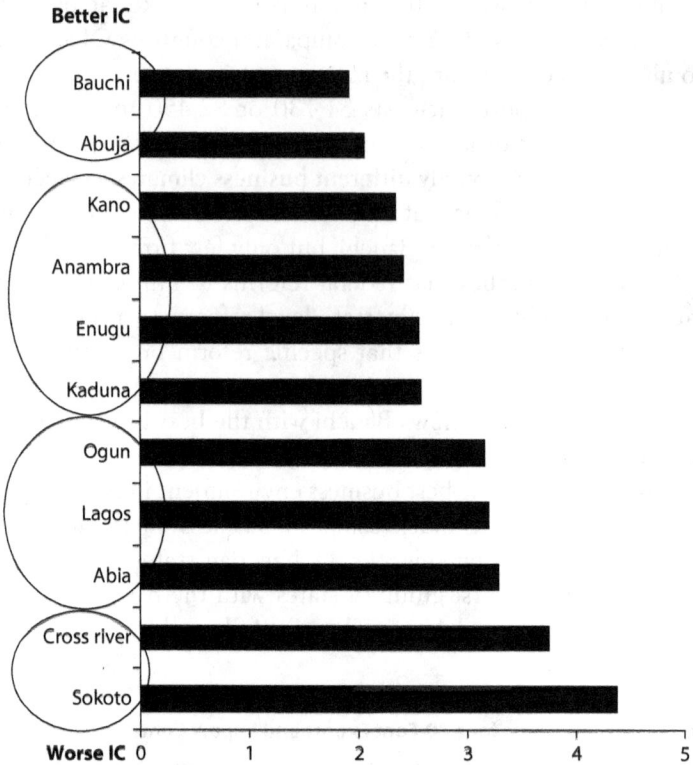

Enugu, and Kaduna. Ogun, Lagos, and Abia show a lower-quality investment climate. And finally the worst investment climate is found in Cross
River and Sokoto.

   **Although some states will benefit more than others from federal
reforms, each state should tackle its own state-level constraints to
improve its business climate.** Our study identified which three reforms
would have the biggest impact in each state (see table 1). Our analysis
shows that when the same federal reforms are implemented in each state,
some states will benefit more than others. Consequently to maximize the
benefit of reforms on the business environment, states must complement
the federal reforms on energy, finance, and transport with state-specific
reforms. Abia, Bauchi, Enugu, Lagos, and Ogun should implement
reforms on access to land. Abuja should address issues of corruption and
improve access to water, Ogun state should improve vertical integration
across firms, and Anambra should improve tax administration.

Table 1   Three Most Important State Reforms to Improve the ICI

Abia	Abuja
1. Cost of short-term finance	1. Cost of short-term finance
2. Transport	2. Bribes for gavernment contract
3. Access to land	3. Water
Anaibra	**Bauchi**
1. Cost of short-term finance	1. Transport
2. Electricity	2. Electricity
3. Tax evasion	3. Access to land
Cross River	**Enugu**
1. Cost of short-term finance	1. Cost of short-term finance
2. Transport	2. Transport
3. Electricity	3. Access to land
Kaduna	**Kano**
1. Cost of short-term finance	1. Cost of short-term finance
2. Transport	2. Access to finance
3. Electricity	3. Electricity
Lagos	**Ogun**
1. Cost of short-term finance	1. Cost of short-term finance
2. Access to finance	2. Access to land
3. Access to land	3. Sales as intermediate products
Sokoto	
1. Cost of short-term finance	
2. Access to finance	
3. Electricity	

Informal firms and female entrepreneurs will also benefit from these reforms. Finally the report shows that micro firms and female entrepreneurs in Nigeria face the same constraints identified by other firms. Micro firms prefer to stay in the informal sector because of the high regulatory burden. They find it difficult to get information on how to register, and once they do have the information, they are deterred by what is still considered a complex and time-consuming process, notwithstanding the significant "streamlining" reforms that have been implemented by the Corporate Affairs Commission in the past few years.

CHAPTER 1

Firm Productivity in Nigeria

Manufacturing Productivity Has Declined in Recent Years

During the past decade Nigeria's manufacturing sector has stagnated as productivity (measured in value added per worker) lagged behind that of many comparator countries. A UNIDO study revealed that the productivity of Nigerian workers was only 10 percent of that in Botswana and 50 percent of that in Ghana and Kenya.[1] The deterioration of the manufacturing sector in recent years can be attributed to a number of factors, including a poor investment climate and low capacity utilization. Average capacity utilization in the manufacturing sector declined from a peak of nearly 80 percent in 1978 to less than 30 percent in the 1990s before rising marginally at the end of the decade. It still hovers at about 65 percent.

This chapter analyzes the performance of Nigerian enterprises using different measures of productivity. The analysis is based on a survey of 2,387 firms[2] conducted by the World Bank through its 2007 Investment Climate project in Nigeria.[3] Nigerian firms are benchmarked to those in other comparator countries in Africa and elsewhere. Productivity differentials across firm size, sectors, and states are explored. The chapter also explores the link between productivity and employment, and allocative efficiency.

Labor Cost and Labor Productivity in Nigeria

Labor cost is one indicator often used to assess the competitive position of a country. When comparing labor cost in Nigeria with that of other countries we observe that Nigeria enjoys lower labor costs than South Africa, Brazil, and Kenya but higher costs than India and Indonesia. Given that total labor costs mask significant variation across different labor skills, we also estimated the labor cost by skills categories. Not surprisingly labor costs are higher for higher skilled workers. Even so, South Africa, Brazil, and Kenya appear to have relatively high labor costs in each labor category [4] (figure 1.1).

But labor cost in itself is only an imperfect indicator of competitiveness. Labor productivity is also an important factor. We use the concept of value added per worker to measure labor productivity.[5] Our results indicate that the average value added per worker in the manufacturing sector is approximately $3,980 (table 1.1).[6] Beneath the aggregate numbers there is wide variation across firm grouping, such as sector and location.

Figure 1.1   Annual Labor Cost (LC) for Skilled and Unskilled Workers

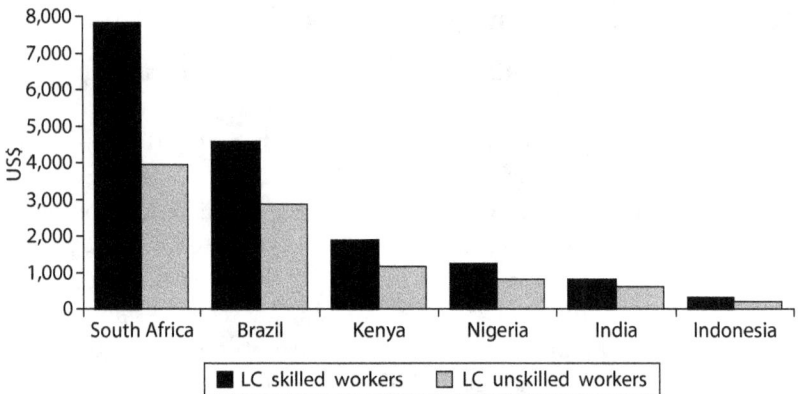

Table 1.1   Productivity in Nigerian Firms

	Value Added/ Worker ($)	Unit Labor Cost (share)
Total Mfg	3,980	0.36
Food	4,172	0.37
Garment	2,977	0.48
Other Mfg	4,253	0.40
Retail	4,358	0.28
Rest of services	3,454	0.26

Source: World Bank, Investment Climate Survey for Nigeria 2007.

The labor productivity of large firms is much higher than that of smaller firms. This finding is consistent across many countries. It is not surprising, because the tough business environment in Nigeria appears to penalize smaller firms more than larger firms. For instance, although large firms would be able to afford private power generators to miti-gate the effects of power outages on production activities, smaller firms are less able to do so. Similarly, complex and complicated sets of busi-ness regulations are likely to exert a considerable drag on the operations of smaller firms.

The retail sector has the highest labor productivity ($4,358), followed closely by food processing and other manufacturing sectors (figure 1.2). The garment sector has the lowest value added per worker, and it is not surprising to learn that most of the domestic garment sector has closed down in recent years.

How does productivity vary across Nigerian states? Firms from 11 states were included in the survey, and the results show that when all firms are included in the analysis, average value added per worker is high-est in Lagos ($6,740), followed by Ogun ($5,170) and Nigeria's capital city ($5,038) (figure 1.3). Three other states (Sokoto, Kano, and Kaduna) have registered labor productivity greater than $3,000.

International Comparison of Value Added per Worker

Benchmarking Nigerian firms against international comparators provides an insight into the nature and extent of the international competitive-ness of Nigerian firms (table 1.2).[7] The table reveals that Nigeria, with an

Figure 1.2   Productivity by Sector

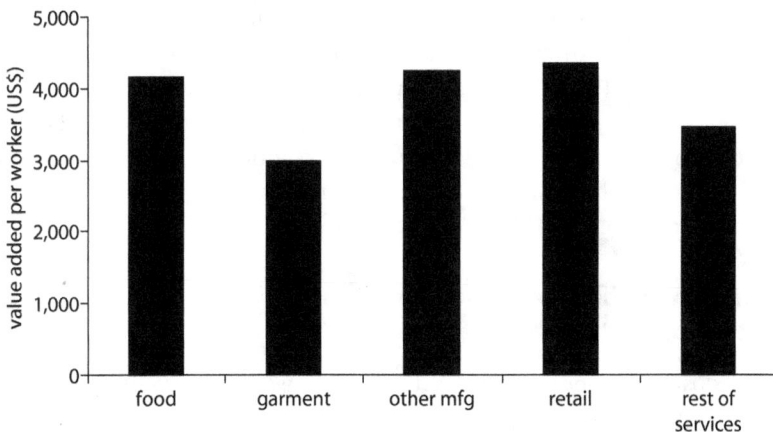

Figure 1.3   Value Added per Worker by State

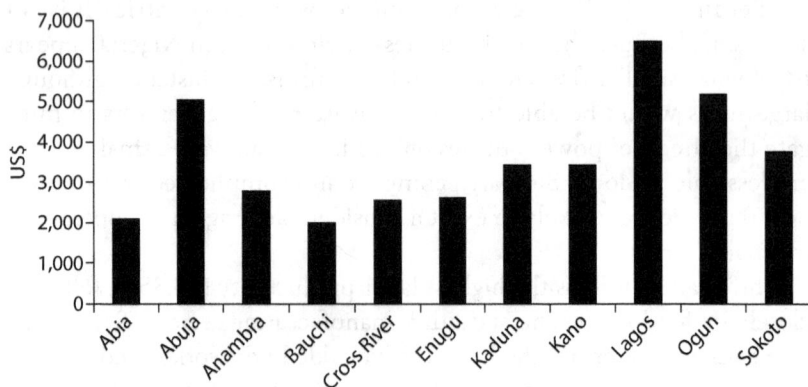

Table 1.2   Productivity—International Comparison

	Mean Value Added Per Worker (US$'000)
Brazil, 2003	13.504
China, 2002	11.607
India, 2005	3.555
Indonesia, 2003	2.986
Kenya, 2007	13.078
Nigeria, 2007	**3.980**
South Africa, 2003	24.938

average value added per worker of $3,980, has the third lowest labor pro-ductivity (after Indonesia and India). South African firms in 2003, recorded the highest value added per employee of $24,938. Brazil ranked second with $13,504, followed by China ($11,607) and Kenya ($13,078).

The aggregate data, however, mask considerable variation across firm groupings. South Africa has the highest value added per employee in all three categories (small, medium, and large firms) (figure 1.4).

More than 90 percent of Nigerian firms are small-size enterprises with low employment, fragmented production activities, and limited access to finance and technology. Also, capacity utilization of Nigerian firms is the lowest among comparator countries (figure 1.5).

Combining Labor Costs and Labor Productivity: Unit Labor Costs

Labor costs and labor productivity taken in isolation give only a partial picture of a country's competitive position. Even if labor costs are

Figure 1.4   Value Added per Worker by Country and Size

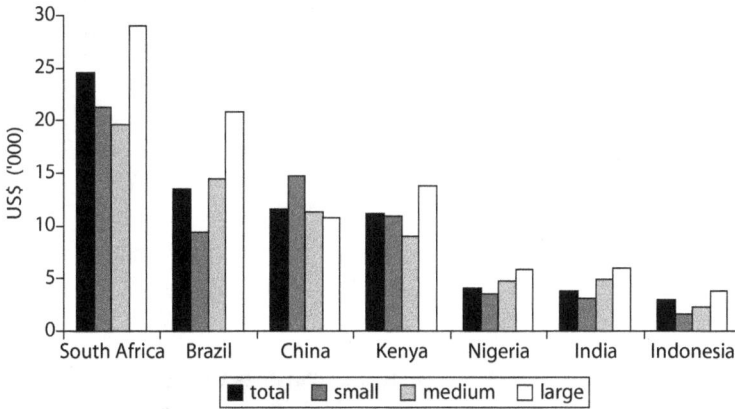

Figure 1.5   Capacity Utilization in Selected Countries

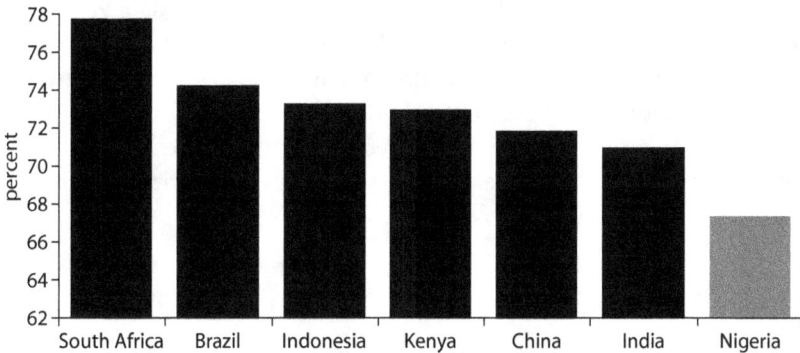

high, a country can be competitive as long as labor productivity is high. Consequently the extent to which a country is competitive depends on both labor costs and labor productivity. We analyze this in Nigeria by looking at the ratio of labor costs over labor productivity: the unit labor cost.

Table 1.3 shows the ratio of wages to value added for Nigeria and comparator countries. Nigeria's 2006 unit labor cost is better than that for Kenya (2007) and South Africa (2003) and similar to that for Brazil (2003). But Nigeria is less competitive than India (2002) and Indonesia (2003). This suggests that Nigeria has the potential to be competitive in the international arena. Nonetheless, it is evident that the ratio of wages to value added has increased, resulting in a deterioration in competitiveness over the years.

Table 1.3   Labor Cost and Unit Labor Cost—International Comparison

	Year	Ratio of Wages-to-Value Added (%)	Labor Cost (US$)
Brazil	2003	0.424	3,827
India	2005	0.237	806
Indonesia	2003	0.091	335
Kenya	2007	0.486	3,598
Nigeria	**2007**	**0.36**	1,466
South Africa	2003	0.447	9,947

Source: World Bank, Investment Climate Survey Nigeria 2007.

A World Bank assessment of the private sector conducted in 2002 reported that Nigeria had a relatively low ratio of wages to value added but that the ratio has risen over the years, from 0.20 in 1983 to 0.26 in 2001 (World Bank 2002). It appears that this rising trend in unit labor cost continues to gain momentum; the 2007 ICA survey data yielded an average wage-value added ratio of 0.36. One of the explanations for this phenomenon is that growth in nominal wages has outpaced growth in productivity during the past two decades or so, and that wage levels in the Nigerian manufacturing sector have remained substantially above those in many of the comparator countries, particularly in Asia (World Bank 2002).

Productivity and Employment

Given that the productivity of labor is an important determinant in explaining the productivity of the overall economy, there is a clear link between employment levels and productivity. In any economy we would expect that increasing productivity would result in increasing demand for labor. When we apply the proposition above to the Nigerian data, we find that a 1 percent increase in productivity (measured as total factor productivity) leads to a 0.41 percent increase in employment.[8] There is therefore clear evidence that improving firm performance can have a positive effect on employment in the country. This finding calls for concerted efforts by the Nigerian authorities to improve the investment climate and thereby realize productivity gains that would stimulate additional employment creation.[9] As a matter of fact, earlier studies[10] have shown that an adverse business environment can impose substantial indirect costs on firms, depressing revenues and hence productivity.

Linking Productive Efficiency to Allocative Efficiency

The competitiveness of a country can be influenced at two levels: productive efficiency at the firm level and allocative efficiency at the industry level. The former encompasses the concepts of labor productivity and total factor productivity of the firm, and the latter focuses on ways of reallocating resources across sector, firm size, and regions, so that more productive firms obtain higher shares of the market. The analysis in this chapter has so far focused on the productive efficiency of firms in Nigeria and not on allocative efficiency. What is the nature and pattern of allocative efficiency in Nigeria and how can it be influenced to enhance productive efficiency of firms?

By using the conventional approach, aggregate productivity can be decomposed into the average productivity of industry and the allocative efficiency component, which is often measured by the covariance between market share of individual firms in a given industry and their productivity (Olley and Pakes 1996). A positive covariance provides evidence of the existence of allocative efficiency, whereas a negative covariance portends allocative inefficiency. Thus a small positive covariance implies that productivity could be enhanced by allocating a higher market share to more productive firms.[11]

Figure 1.6 and Figure 1.7 illustrate the covariance between market share and productivity by firm size and industry in Nigeria. Despite the positive covariance between market share and labor productivity in Nigeria, the magnitudes of such covariances are low, suggesting that more can be done to improve the country's competitiveness. This calls

Figure 1.6   Covariance between Labor Productivity and Market Share

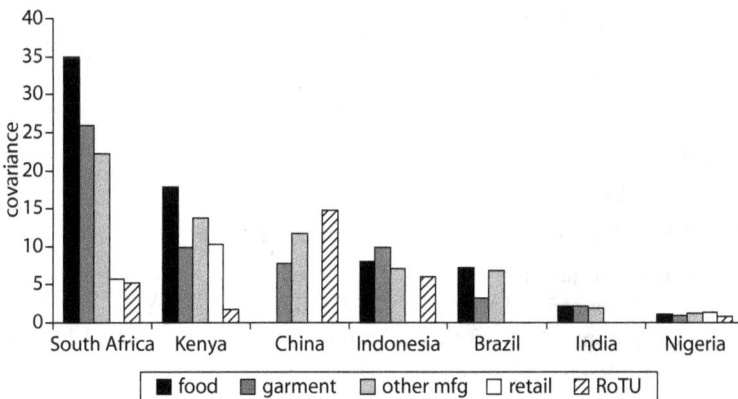

Figure 1.7   Covariance between Labor Productivity and Market Share

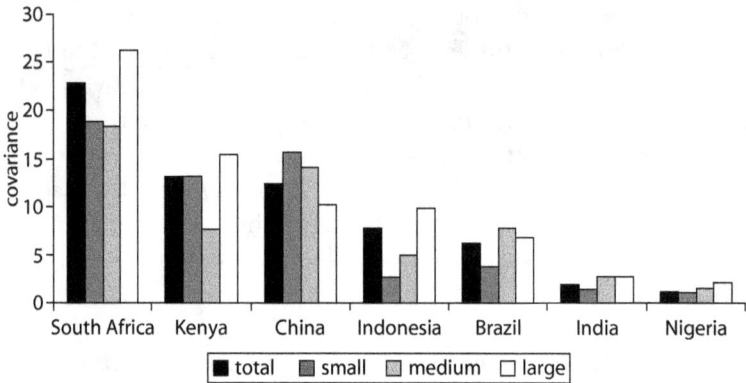

for a positive and proactive intervention at two levels: macro and micro. At the macro level, allocative efficiency could be improved by enabling more productive firms to obtain a higher share of the market through the elimination of obstacles to competition, for example by reducing barriers to entry, making it easier to register property and to trade across borders. At the micro level, however, allocative efficiency could be improved on two fronts, external as well as internal to the firm. On the external side, there is need to improve the business environment. Removing constraints to doing business in Nigeria is likely to raise productivity and create jobs, which could in turn boost incomes and alleviate poverty. Internally, firms need to improve the way they are managed, as econometric analysis suggests that managerial ability contributes positively to both labor productivity and total factor productivity in Nigeria. All these issues are covered in the following chapters.

Notes

1. Soderbom and Teal 2002.
2. See appendix for sample description.
3. The World Bank Group-DFID State Level Investment Climate Program.
4. Labor cost and unit labor cost are often used to assess the relative competitiveness of countries. Labor cost is calculated by dividing total employer's costs (total compensation) by total number of employees. Unit labor cost is defined as the ratio of total wage bill to value added.

5. We opt for value added, defined as sales minus total raw materials, to allow for comparison with previous assessment of Nigeria's private sector performance (World Bank, RPED Nigeria 2002).

6. The analysis in this chapter excludes firms with outlier observations. Thus, the mean values reported here are "trimmed" means, which exclude 10 percent of most extreme values (outliers).

7. The survey results across countries have revealed outliers, which have subsequently been removed from the analysis. Hence the descriptive statistics present here are based on the trimmed means.

8. Because labor productivity depends also on capital available, a broader measure of productivity often used is that of total factor productivity (TFP). This is an indicator of productivity that takes into account both labor and capital used in the production process. See appendix in ICA study for more details.

9. See Appendix for more details.

10. See *The World Development Report 2004* and Eifert, Gelb, and Ramachandran (2008).

11. For a detailed analysis of the methodological approach and its application, see Escribano and Guasch (2005).

CHAPTER 2

The Business Environment in Nigeria

Indirect Costs of Doing Business in Nigeria Are High

An adverse business environment can increase production costs substantially. It is estimated that the manufacturing sector in Nigeria has to bear additional indirect costs amounting to 16 percent of sales because of bottlenecks in the business environment. Losses due to power outages amount to 10 percent of sales, and production lost while in transit (4 percent of sales) is also significant (see table 2.1). These losses affect different types of firms in different ways. Electricity is more of a problem for small and medium-size firms. Production lost while in transit affects large firms to a greater extent.

In comparison with other countries, we can see from figure 2.1 that firms in Nigeria face higher indirect costs than firms in all other comparators. This is due largely to electricity-related losses. By contrast, Nigerian firms have similar indirect costs resulting from corruption and crime.

Electricity, Finance, and Transport Are the Major Perceived Constraints

To identify the main bottlenecks the Investment Climate Survey asked Nigeria's managers about the major constraints to doing business. Three

Table 2.1 Indirect Costs—Manufacturing Sector

| Indirect costs as % sales | TOTAL | Exporting zone | | Firm size | | | Ownership | | State | |
		Yes	No	Small	Med.	Large	Foreign	Domestic	More industrialized	Less industrialized
Electricity	**9.8**	9.3	9.9	10.2	9.3	5.3	10.3	9.8	9.8	9.7
Bribes	**1.7**	2.8	1.5	1.5	2.2	0.9	0.4	1.7	1.7	1.6
Production lost while in transit	**4.1**	7.3	3.6	3.3	5.2	11.6	1.7	4.2	3.8	4.9
Theft, robbery, or arson	**0.3**	0.3	0.4	0.3	0.4	0.4	0.3	0.3	0.3	0.5
Total indirect costs	**15.9**	19.7	15.3	15.3	17.2	18.3	12.7	16.0	15.6	16.8

Source: ICA Survey.

Figure 2.1   Indirect Costs—Manufacturing Sector—International Comparison

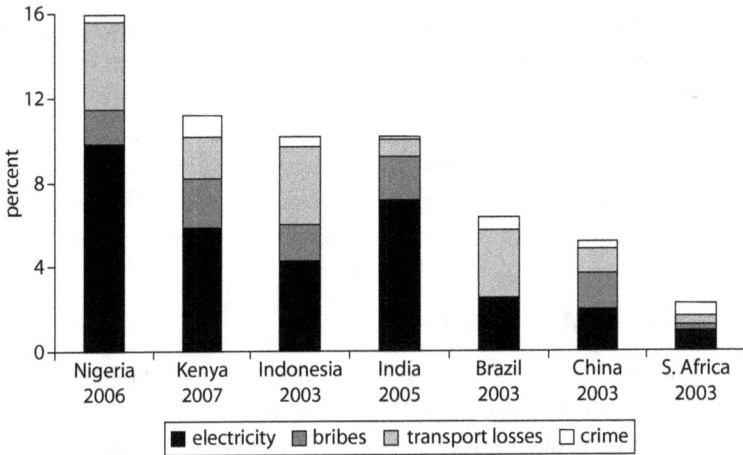

Source: Investment Climate Survey in Nigeria.

Figure 2.2   Electricity, Finance, and Transport Are Major Perceived Constraints

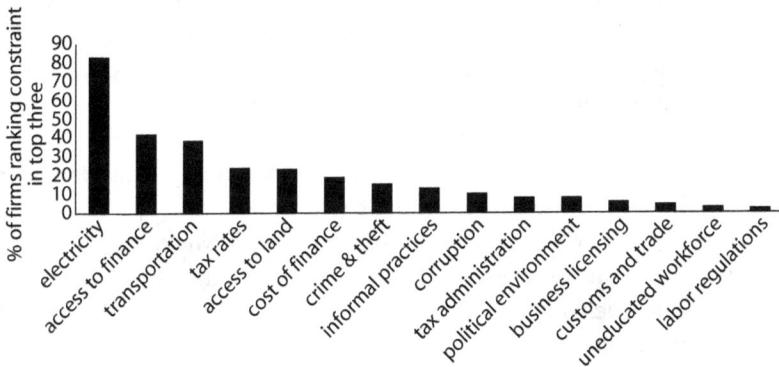

Source: Investment Climate Survey in Nigeria.

major constraints emerged; electricity, finance, and transportation. (figure 2.2) The perception of other obstacles varies across firms. Although electricity appears to be a challenge for all firms, its impact is more significant in the manufacturing sector. Access to and the cost of finance appear to affect small and medium firms more significantly than they affect large firms, as well as firms located in the less industrialized states. Domestic firms complain significantly more of access to finance than do foreign firms.

In the manufacturing sector, more than 50 percent of firms perceive electricity, access to finance, and cost of finance as the three most important constraints to their operations; transportation, the macroeconomic environment, access to land, tax rates, corruption, and crime appear as second-tier concerns (table 2.2).

In benchmarking Nigeria internationally, figure 2.3 shows that electricity, finance, transport, and access to land appear to be serious constraints when compared with other countries. By contrast, Nigeria's entrepreneurs do not perceive corruption, crime, and tax rates to be obstacles.

Electricity: The Main Bottleneck

In Nigeria power outages result in losses equivalent to 10 percent of total sales. Almost all Nigerian firms (97 percent) experience power outages. On average, such outages lasted some 196 hours per month, that is, approximately 8 days. Large firms and firms in the manufacturing sector are more adversely affected by such outages.

Faced with this situation, 86 percent of firms have their own generators, which produce, on average, 61 percent of their electricity needs. (table 2.3) Large firms have lower electricity-related indirect costs although they face the most significant outages. This is explained by the fact that 97 percent of them have their own generators. Power outages vary by state. In Kano, total outage duration averages 393 hours per month, equivalent to 16 days. In Abuja, total outage duration averages 127 hours per month, equivalent to 5 days.

In comparison with other countries (table 2.4), we can see that the percentage of firms experiencing power outages is highest in Nigeria. As a consequence, generator ownership is also higher in Nigeria than in all other comparators.

Transportation and Customs

Transportation emerged as the third most important major constraint to business. Transportation problems generate indirect costs due to breakage, spoilage, or theft, in the order of 4 percent of total sales (see table 2.1), making it the second most important indirect cost driver behind electricity. The main cause of such costs is breakage or spoilage (3.2 percent) while in transit. This should not be surprising given the very small share of roads in Nigeria that are paved (estimated at about 15 percent in 2004 compared with 80 percent of China). And yet road transport remains a

Table 2.2 Percentage of Firms Reporting Major or Very Severe Constraints—Manufacturing Sector

| Constraint | TOTAL | Exporting zone | | Firm size | | | Ownership | | State | | State | |
		Yes	No	Small	Med.	Large	Foreign	Dom.	More industrialized	Less industrialized	Better regulatory environment	Worse regulatory environment
Electricity	**81%**	78%	81%	82%	79%	76%	100%	81%	79%	84%	85%	76%
Access to finance (e.g., collateral)	**56%**	33%	60%	65%	37%	14%	32%	56%	53%	63%	59%	52%
Cost of finance (e.g., interest rates)	**50%**	36%	53%	58%	34%	23%	66%	50%	48%	57%	55%	45%
Transportation	**33%**	24%	35%	32%	35%	29%	70%	33%	30%	40%	28%	39%
Macroeconomic environment	**30%**	28%	30%	27%	37%	25%	25%	30%	33%	22%	29%	31%
Access to land for expansion/ relocation	**29%**	19%	30%	32%	21%	19%	58%	28%	27%	33%	32%	25%
Tax rates	**27%**	18%	28%	27%	27%	13%	32%	26%	26%	29%	36%	16%
Corruption	**24%**	8%	27%	28%	17%	9%	36%	24%	24%	26%	33%	14%
Crime, theft, and disorder	**20%**	17%	21%	22%	17%	11%	25%	20%	19%	24%	20%	20%

(continued)

Table 2.2 Percentage of Firms Reporting Major or Very Severe Constraints—Manufacturing Sector (Continued)

Constraint	TOTAL	Exporting zone		Firm size			Ownership		State		State	
		Yes	No	Small	Med.	Large	Foreign	Dom.	More industrialized	Less industrialized	Better regulatory environment	Worse regulatory environment
Practices of competitors in informal sector	**19%**	20%	19%	21%	15%	9%	34%	19%	20%	18%	22%	16%
Tax administration	**18%**	20%	17%	18%	18%	2%	32%	17%	17%	18%	22%	13%
Business licensing and permits	**14%**	14%	14%	16%	12%	0%	13%	14%	11%	22%	17%	12%
Political environment	**13%**	9%	13%	13%	13%	0%	25%	13%	13%	12%	20%	5%
Inadequately educated workforce	**6%**	10%	5%	6%	6%	2%	20%	5%	5%	8%	7%	4%
Telecommunications	**5%**	2%	6%	6%	5%	3%	20%	5%	3%	11%	7%	3%
Labor regulations	**5%**	9%	5%	5%	6%	0%	13%	5%	5%	5%	9%	2%
Customs and trade regulations	**4%**	10%	3%	3%	7%	1%	13%	4%	5%	4%	5%	3%

Source: ICA Survey.

Figure 2.3   Top Constraints in Nigeria—International Comparison

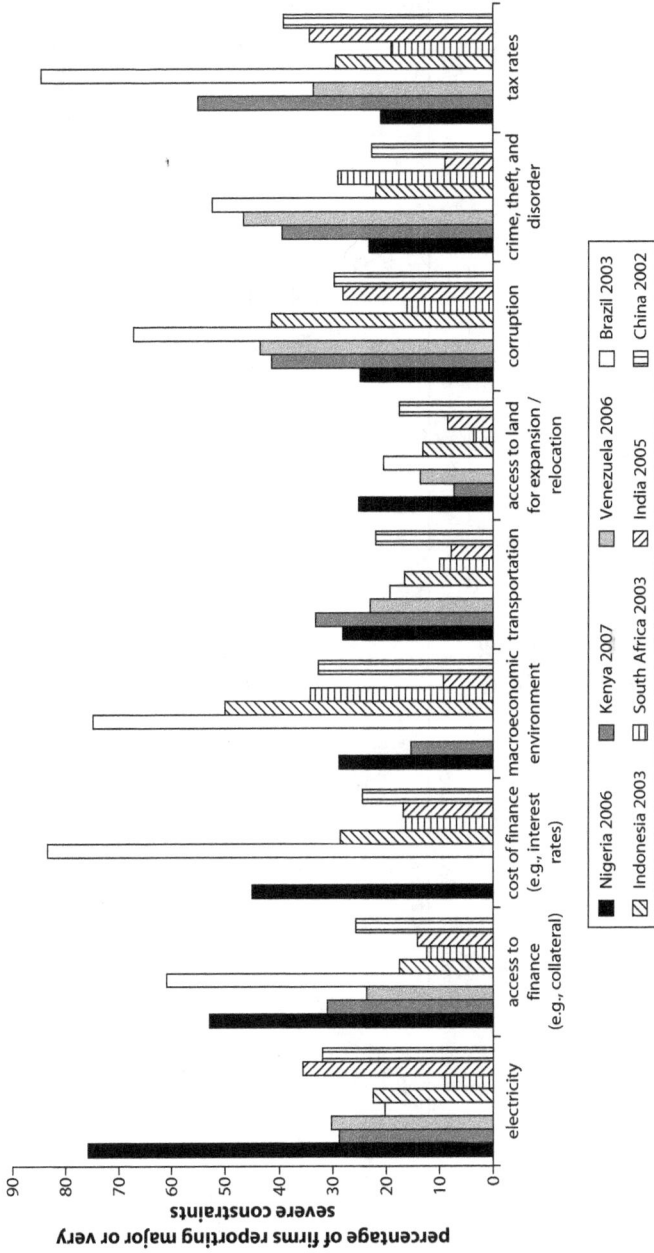

Source: Investment Climate Survey in Nigeria.

Table 2.3 Infrastructure Indicators—All Formal Sectors

Indicator	TOTAL	Firm size			Ownership		Industry			State	
		Small	Med.	Large	Foreign	Dom.	Manuf.	Retail	Other	More industrialized	Less industrialized
% firms experienced power outages	**96**	96	95	100	92	96	98	96	93	97	93
Average duration of outages per month (hours)	**196**	198	186	223	125	197	238	188	150	212	169
% firms with own generator	**86**	84	99	97	86	86	86	85	92	87	84
% electricity coming from own generator	**61**	61	61	61	70	61	61	N/A	N/A	63	55

Source: ICA Survey.

Table 2.4   Nigerian Businesses Face the Most Serious Electricity Constraints

Indicator	Nigeria 2006	Kenya 2007	Venezuela 2006	Brazil 2003	Indonesia 2003	South Africa 2003	India 2005	China 2003
% firms experienced power outages	96	85	21	64	48	N/A	77	N/A
% firms with own generator	86	70	N/A	17	39	10	59	19

Source: ICA Surveys.

major means to supply factories. Almost 70 percent of manufacturing firms in Nigeria have their inputs delivered by road.

Nigerian firms import 10 percent of their inputs, with large firms (15 percent) and particularly foreign firms (39 percent) importing more. Efficient customs are important for firms that use a significant proportion of inputs from abroad. Only 16 percent of firms import directly, and it takes them approximately 13 days for imports to clear customs. Exporting is a speedier process taking on average seven days to clear customs. In comparison with other countries, the number of days needed to clear customs is clearly high. Brazil and India report waiting times to clear customs approximately equivalent to that of Nigeria, whereas Indonesia, South Africa, and China report clearly lower waiting times (less than eight days) (figure 2.4).

Nigeria does not compare well with other countries in regard to customs clearance, and more specifically for both the import licensing process and the time taken to clear customs. No comparator country requires more documents for both importing and exporting than does Nigeria (figure 2.5)

Finally of all comparator countries Nigeria remains the most expensive location from which to ship imports or exports. To ship a 40-foot container for export, it costs $1,730 and for import it costs $2,450 (see figure 2.6).

In summary, transportation emerges as an important constraint because it generates significant indirect costs of doing business. Although customs and trade regulations are perceived by only 5 percent of firms to be a major or very severe obstacle, this is in all likelihood connected with the relatively low number of firms in Nigeria that are familiar with the customs procedures. For those that do trade, customs appears to be a significant obstacle to business, in both costs and time.

Figure 2.4   Customs—Manufacturing Sector—International Comparison

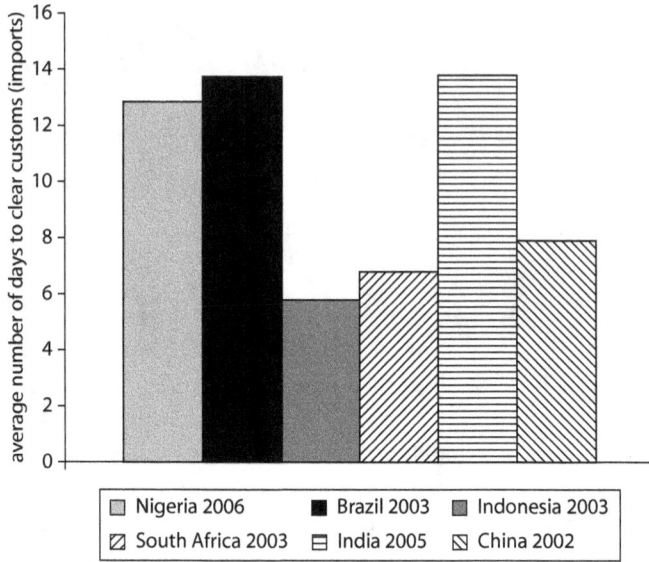

Source: Investment Climate Survey in Nigeria.

Figure 2.5   Trading across Borders—International Comparison

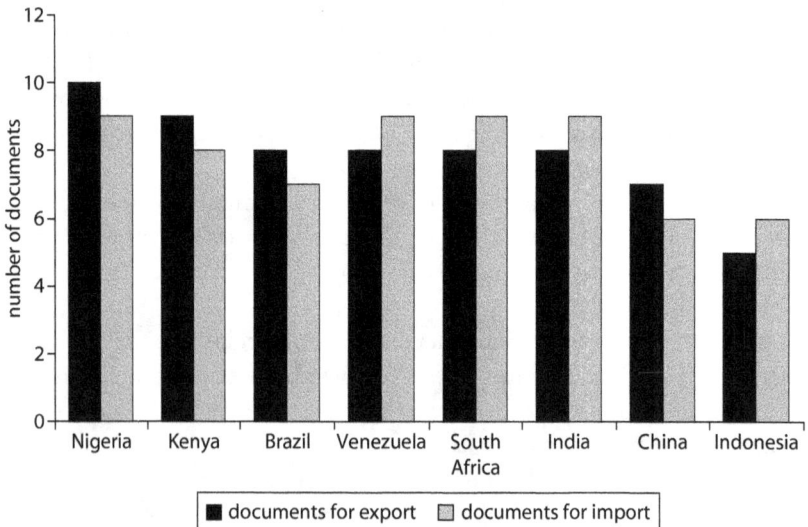

Source: World Bank Doing Business Indicators 2006.

Figure 2.6   Typical Charge for a 40-Foot Export and Import Container

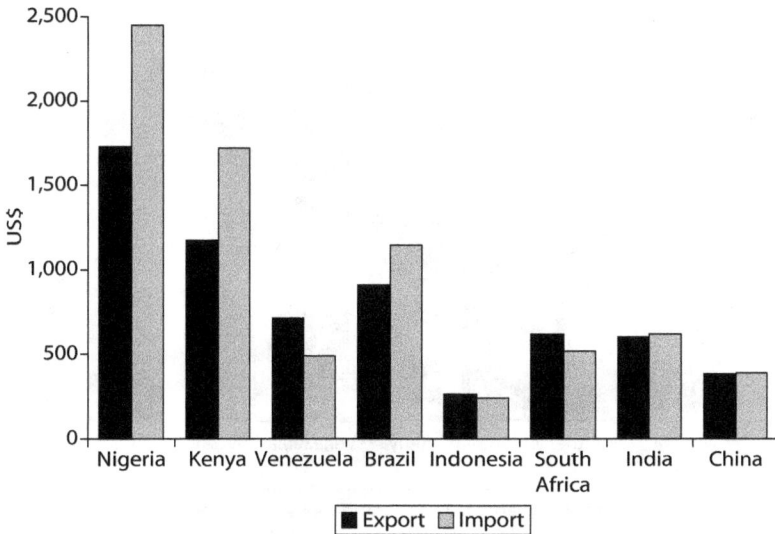

Source: World Bank Doing Business Indicators 2006.

Taxes

All around the world, businesses tend to complain about tax rates. Nevertheless in Nigeria, complaints about tax rates are not at the top of the list. About one in five Nigerian firms identified tax rates as a significant constraint to business, ranking it the fourth most important constraint. In international comparisons a higher percentage of firms complain about tax rates in other countries. However, by using the Doing Business database we can see that the overall tax rate paid by firms in Nigeria is the lowest of our comparator countries. And the profit tax rate is lower only in Venezuela (12 percent) (figure 2.7). Hence it appears that tax rates in Nigeria are not a major bottleneck. The reason they appear in the top part of our ranking is that most of our sample is composed by small firms, which enjoy fewer exemptions and have a higher effective marginal rate of taxation.

Access to Land

Access to land was identified by 25 percent of firms as a significant constraint to business, particularly for small firms as well as for foreign firms.

Figure 2.7   Composition of Taxes—International Comparison

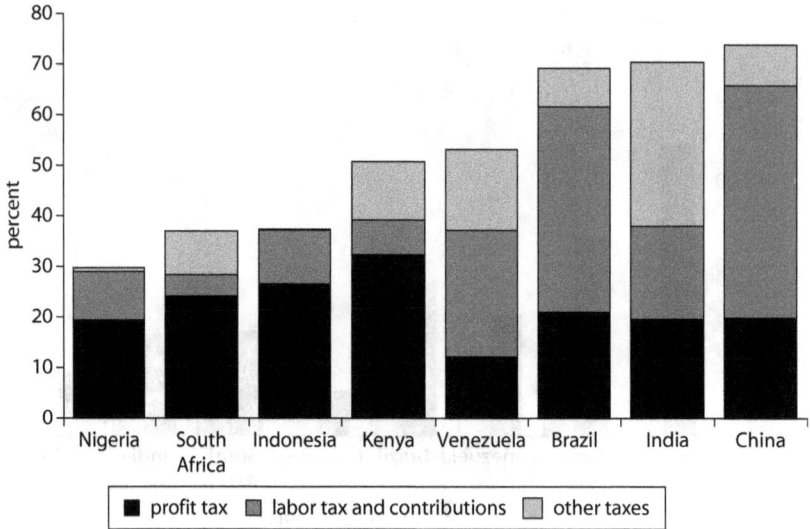

Source: Doing Business.

Table 2.5 takes a closer look at the reasons that may justify this perception. The two main reasons that land is perceived a constraint are, first,
the cost of land and, second, the procurement process.

According to the survey, 25 percent of firms have tried to acquire new
land in the previous three years, and 39 percent of those firms have identified access to land as a major or very severe obstacle. Furthermore,
almost a third of firms that successfully purchased land still report access
to land as a major or very severe obstacle. This suggests that access to land
may indeed be an obstacle; even firms successful in acquiring land identify it as a major or very severe constraint. Although the cost of land
(which is the primary reason that access to land is an obstacle) is an area
in which intervention is difficult, the procurement process could be significantly improved.

Corruption and Crime

Corruption is perceived to be a serious constraint by 25 percent of firms.
In an international comparison, we found that a higher percentage of
comparator countries' firms report corruption to be a serious constraint.
Bribes account for some 2 percent of total sales, which is more or less in
line with the same indicator in comparator countries (see figure 2.1).

Table 2.5 Reasons for Perceiving Access to Land for Expansion/Relocation to Be a Major or Very Severe Constraint—All Formal Sectors

Percentage of firms that identify this as reason for access to land for expansion/relocation to be an obstacle	TOTAL	Firm size			Ownership		Industry			State	
		Small	Med.	Large	Foreign	Dom.	Manuf.	Retail	Other	More industrialized	Less industrialized
Cost of land	**92**	92	90	100	89	92	97	85	88	92	91
Procurement process	**70**	71	68	67	89	70	68	72	72	69	72
Availability of infrastructure	**47**	46	51	29	46	47	47	46	46	45	49
Small size of land ownership	**39**	37	47	49	51	39	32	44	48	34	46
Government ownership of land	**39**	37	45	80	18	39	38	37	43	45	31
Disputed ownership	**35**	33	42	69	53	34	28	32	48	32	39

Source: Investment Climate Survey in Nigeria.
Note: Table includes only firms that perceived access to land to be major or very severe constraint.

Looking in more detail at corruption, table 2.6 shows that only 44 percent of firms believe that government officials have a consistent and predictable interpretation of the law. This uncertainty may be closely linked to corruption. As shown above, small and medium firms perceive corruption to be more of a problem. We can see in table 2.6 that overall some 33 percent of firms report informal payments or gifts to be common to "get things done" in customs, taxes, licenses, regulations, and so on, and only 25 percent know in advance the amount of payment needed. When a government contract is at stake, firms expect to have to pay some 5 percent of its value in such informal gifts or payments to secure it.

Table 2.7 shows the percentage of firms that have been asked for informal payments when making certain requests, such as a telephone or electrical connection or permits and licenses. More than half of all firms have been asked for such informal payments when requesting construction permits and 40 percent when requesting operating licenses. With the exception of construction permits, this problem affects small and medium firms to a greater extent, which may justify their higher perceptions of corruption.

The court system is another institution in which corruption may be a problem. Table 2.8 shows that firms do not have much confidence in it: only half of all firms believe the system to be fair, impartial, and uncorrupted, and only three of four believe the courts to be able to enforce decisions. Clearly, the problem appears to be not so much at the postdecision stage, but at the predecision stage, with almost 60 percent of firms considering the process slow and expensive. This conclusion is reinforced by the fact that although 4 percent of firms had payment disputes in the past two years, only just over half of them were taken to court.

Other sources appear to confirm that although corruption may be perceived as a major bottleneck in Nigeria, it is not much worse than in comparator countries. Transparency International's corruption perceptions index (CPI), which attempts to quantify the degree of corruption as seen by businesspeople and country analysts, ranges between 10 (highly clean) and 0 (highly corrupt). Table 2.9 shows that Nigeria ranks 147th (of 180 countries), close to Indonesia; Kenya and Venezuela appear to be slightly worse.

These results may, at first sight, seem intriguing. Internationally, Nigeria is perceived to be a country in which corruption is a major problem. In fact, the data from table 2.9 do suggest that corruption is (in relative terms) problematic because it ranks Nigeria 147th of 180 countries. However, a closer look at the data shows that corruption

Table 2.6 Perception of Government and Regulations—All Formal Sectors

% firms that agree with statement	TOTAL	Firm size			Ownership		Industry			State	
		Small	Med.	Large	Foreign	Dom.	Manuf.	Retail	Other	More industrialized	Less industrialized
Consistent and predictable interpretation of the law	**44**	39	58	74	40	44	43	46	42	46	39
Informal payments/gifts commonplace	**33**	35	29	24	45	33	31	31	38	31	37
Advance knowledge of informal payment/gift	**25**	26	21	19	26	25	26	22	25	25	24
Percentage of annual sales spent on informal payments/gifts	**2.0**	2.0	2.3	0.7	0.7	2.0	1.7	2.0	2.4	1.7	2.4
Percentage of contract value paid to secure contract	**5.3**	5.6	4.7	2.0	4.8	5.3	5.5	4.0	6.0	4.0	7.5

Source: Investment Climate Survey in Nigeria.

Table 2.7   Percentage of Firms Asked for Informal Payments When Making Requests—All Formal Sectors

% firms that have been asked for informal payments when requesting	TOTAL	Firm size			Ownership		Industry			State	
		Small	Med.	Large	Foreign	Dom.	Manuf.	Retail	Other	More industrialized	Less industrialized
Telephone connection	**24**	27	20	11	58	24	15	32	29	19	36
Electrical connection	**39**	42	32	10	57	39	35	40	43	38	42
Water connection	**33**	35	30	11	68	32	24	42	37	29	39
Construction permit	**53**	51	56	67	79	52	51	42	59	50	57
Import license	**33**	48	12	35	71	31	24	26	65	23	52
Operating license	**40**	47	28	10	53	40	36	42	45	37	46

Source: Investment Climate Survey in Nigeria.

Table 2.8 Court System—All Formal Sectors

Characteristics of the court system	TOTAL	Firm size			Ownership		Industry			State	
		Small	Med.	Large	Foreign	Dom.	Manuf.	Retail	Other	More industrialized	Less industrialized
Fair, impartial, and uncorrupted	**53**	52	57	61	48	54	53	46	59	53	55
Quick	**41**	41	41	54	46	41	38	39	47	42	40
Affordable	**41**	38	49	67	58	41	38	40	45	43	38
Able to enforce decisions	**75**	75	77	84	75	75	75	79	74	75	76
Percentage of firms with payment disputes in the past 2 years settled by third parties	**4**	3	6	6	8	4	3	5	4	4	4

Source: Investment Climate Survey in Nigeria.

37

Table 2.9   Corruption Perceptions Index, 2007

Country	Rank (180 countries)	Index
Nigeria	147	2.2
Kenya	150	2.1
Venezuela	162	2.0
Brazil	72	3.5
Indonesia	143	2.3
South Africa	43	5.1
India	72	3.5
China	72	3.5

Source: Transparency International.

does not appear to be much worse in Nigeria than in the other comparator countries, especially Kenya, Venezuela, and Indonesia. According to
the investment climate survey data fewer firms in Nigeria perceive corruption to be a major or very severe constraint when compared with
Kenya, Venezuela, and Indonesia, which is in line with the perceptions
reported by Transparency International.

It can be argued that managers internalize corruption and hence
report a lower level of corruption even though the problem is actually
higher than perceived. To address this concern we looked instead at
objective indicators of corruption, such as the amount of bribes paid
"to get things done." Even in this case, as shown earlier, objective indicators of corruption show that the amount of bribes paid by firms in
Nigeria is lower than that paid in Kenya and similar to the amount paid
in Indonesia. Furthermore if we look at the evolution of corruption
over time we notice that in the past few years Nigeria's corruption
level has been improving. This finding is confirmed by other sources
and is a result of the significant effort taken by the Nigerian government to fight corruption through enacting the Corrupt Practices Act
and establishing the Independent Corrupt Practices and Other Related
Offences Commission (figure 2.8).

Finally, Transparency International's report on the Global Corruption
Barometer (2007) confirms this assessment. Nigeria appears as a country
in which corruption is (in relative terms) a problem. However, respon-
dents are broadly optimistic and expect corruption to become less of a
problem in the future, and they consider the government's efforts to fight
corruption to be effective.

Hence, our conclusion is that although corruption in Nigeria is a
problem (it continues to rank in the bottom deciles in international

Figure 2.8   Evolution over Time of Nigeria's Percentile Rank for Rule of Law and Control of Corruption

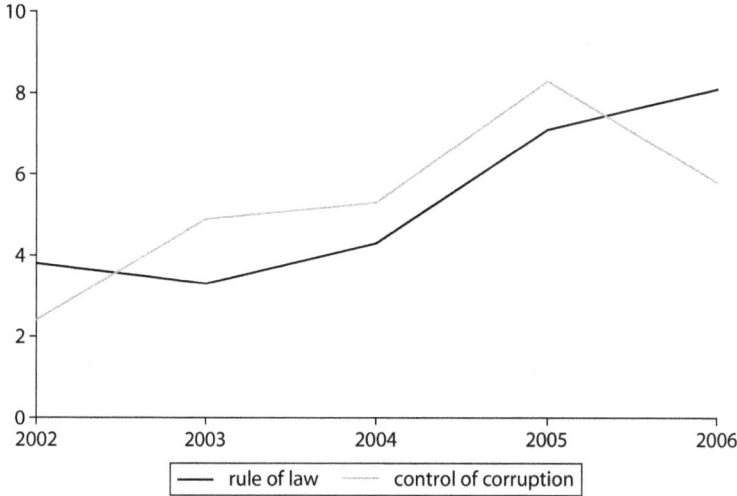

Source: World Bank Governance Indicators.

comparisons), a significant effort has been made to address it, as objective indicators as well as changes in perception over time (both CPI and governance indicators) have shown.

Crime was also reported to be a serious constraint to business by 23 percent of firms. However, crime generates indirect costs of only 0.8 percent of sales, clearly lower than those associated with electricity or even corruption. According to the ICA survey, 20 percent of firms in the formal sector experienced losses as a result of theft, robbery, vandalism, or arson. In an international comparison, with the exception of India, crime is perceived to be a more serious constraint everywhere else than in Nigeria. However, crime generates more or less similar indirect costs as in Nigeria (see figure 2.1).

A side effect of crime is yet another direct cost that would otherwise not be borne by firms: security. In Nigeria almost 70 percent of firms have to pay for security services, and they spend on average 1.8 percent of their annual sales for such services. Large firms appear to bear higher security costs than do small and medium firms (see table 2.10).

In an international comparison, although the share of firms that use security services is pretty much similar across countries, with the exception of only Indonesia and China, the overall cost burden of security

Table 2.10 Security Services and Security Expenditure—All Formal Sectors

	TOTAL	Firm size			Ownership		Industry		Other	State	
		Small	Med.	Large	Foreign	Dom.	Manuf.	Retail		More industrialized	Less industrialized
Percentage of firms that paid for security services	**69**	65	84	100	100	69	72	66	68	72	65
Security cost as % annual sales	**1.8**	1.8	1.8	2.6	2.6	1.8	2.1	1.3	1.9	1.8	1.9

Source: Investment Climate Survey in Nigeria.

Table 2.11   Security Services and Security Expenditure—Comparison across Countries—All Formal Sectors

	Nigeria 2006	Kenya 2007	Venezuela 2006	Brazil 2003	Indonesia 2003	South Africa 2003	India 2005	China 2002
Percentage of firms that paid for security services	69	70	75	81	46	81	66	48
Security cost as % annual sales	1.8	1.9	6.6	1.6	1.1	0.9	1.3	0.7

Source: Investment Climate Survey in Nigeria.

services paid by Nigerian firms is among the highest, at the same level as Kenya, in which security is a major concern. Venezuela is an outlier (see table 2.11).

This leads us to conclude that although crime is not in the group of the most important constraints, survey data show that it remains a significant obstacle to doing business in Nigeria with significant cost implications.

CHAPTER 3

Comparing the State-Level Investment Climate

While other chapters analyzed Nigeria's investment climate and compared it with that of other countries in Africa and beyond, this chapter benchmarks the investment climate at the state level in the following states: Abia, Abuja, Anambra, Bauchi, Cross River, Enugu, Kaduna, Kano, Lagos, Ogun, and Sokoto.

Which state in Nigeria has the best investment climate? The answer to this question depends on which indicator of the investment climate is examined because there is considerable variation across states in the perception indicators as well as objective variables. Figure 3.1 shows the average perception of each of the main identified constraints, as well as the range across states. For instance, 93 percent of firms in Anambra perceive electricity to be a significant constraint compared with only 69 percent in Lagos and Sokoto. The variation across states is even greater when we look at the cost of finance, access to land, and tax rates. More than three-quarters of firms in Bauchi perceive the cost of finance to be a significant constraint compared with only 20 percent in Sokoto. By contrast, very few firms in Sokoto and Ogun (6 percent and 9 percent, respectively) identify access to land as a significant constraint compared with 56 percent in Abia. Finally, few firms in Lagos and Sokoto (7 percent and 8 percent, respectively) perceive tax rates as a constraint to their businesses, but this figure rises to 54 percent in Kano.

Figure 3.1   Variation across States of the Percentage of Firms Reporting Major or Very Severe Constraints—All Formal Sectors

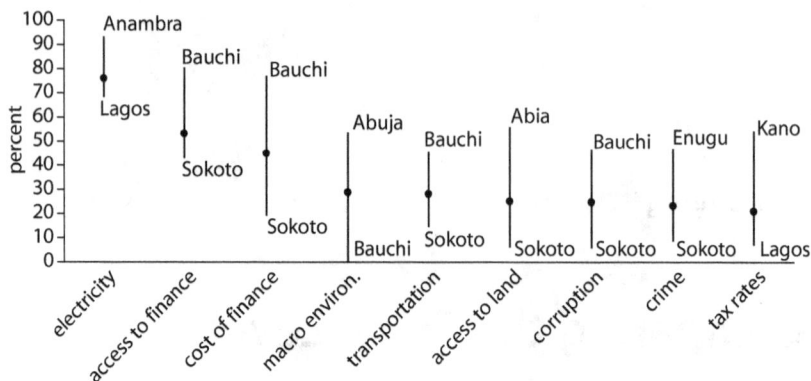

Source: Investment Climate Survey in Nigeria.

Figure 3.2   Indirect Costs: Manufacturing Sector—Comparison across States

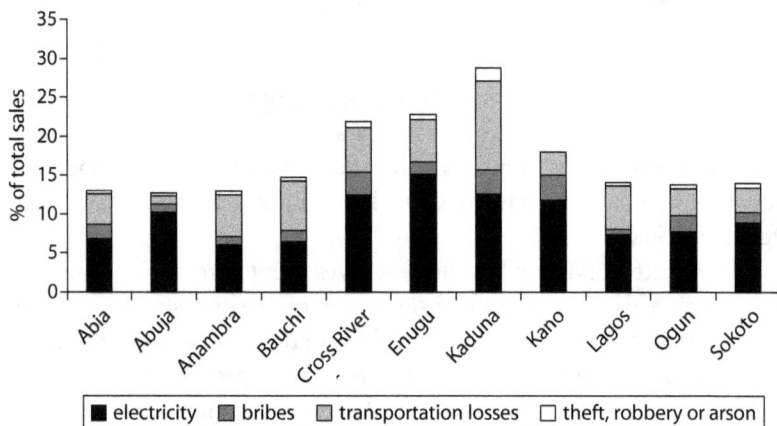

legend: ■ electricity   ■ bribes   ■ transportation losses   □ theft, robbery or arson

If we look at objective indicators, such as indirect costs, the variation across states is similar (figure 3.2). The lowest indirect costs are found in Abuja (13 percent of total sales) and the highest in Kaduna (approximately 29 percent of total sales).

Given this variability and given the broad nature of the investment climate concept, to compare the investment climate in the 11 Nigerian states surveyed we need to construct a composite index. This enables us to summarize in one indicator the many different features of the investment climate in Nigeria, from infrastructure, to inputs, to institutions. In building this composite indicator, which we call the investment climate index (ICI), we use 44 variables concerning cost and quality of infrastructure, inputs, and institutions.[1]

Analysis of the Investment Climate in 11 Nigerian States

Using our composite index we arrive at the ranking displayed in figure 3.3. When reading this ranking it is important to remember that the ICI, as any index, is useful in highlighting broad patterns, but should not be taken as an indicator of the exact position of any individual state.[2] Values that are very close to each other cannot be considered as representing the exact position of a state. For instance the difference between Ogun, Lagos, and Abia is so small that we conclude that these three states have the same quality of investment climate.

Figure 3.3   Investment Climate Index in 11 Nigerian States

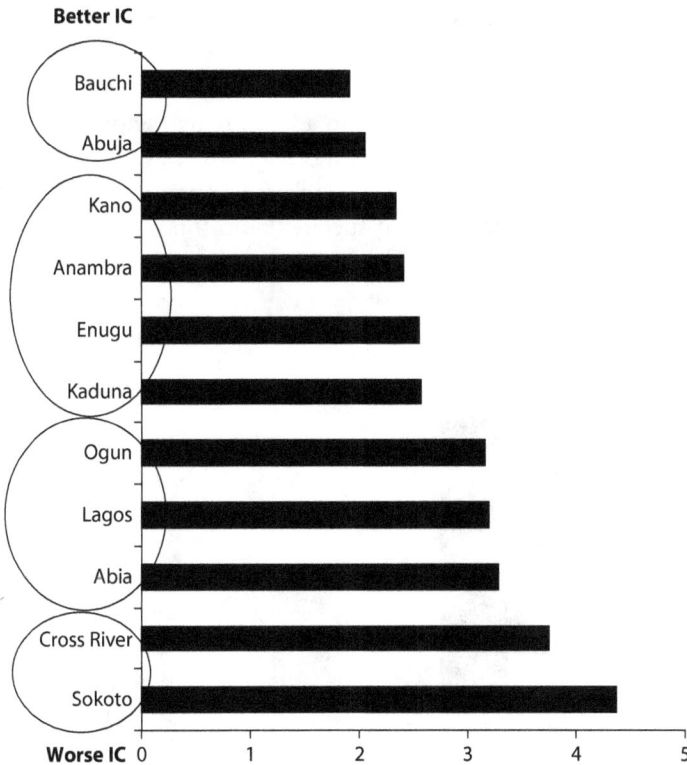

According to the ICI ranking of figure 3.3 the 11 Nigerian states can be classified into four groups. The first group of states with the best investment climate includes Bauchi and Abuja. They are followed by Kano, Anambra, Enugu, and Kaduna. Then Ogun, Lagos, and Abia show a lower investment climate quality. And finally the most challenging investment climates are found in Cross River and Sokoto.

Although individual state ranking is interesting in itself, the purpose of this ranking is not to name which is best or worst, but rather to identify where opportunities for reforms exist. What features of the investment climate make some states more business friendly than others? Why do less industrialized states have a poor business climate? Should states with a weaker regulatory environment concentrate only on improving business regulations to improve their investment climate?

The methodology used to build the composite indicator enables us to isolate which groups of variables have the biggest impact on the investment climate. By decomposing the ICI we can see that the main drivers to a better business environment are represented by variables associated with infrastructure (figure 3.4). Less important are inputs and institutions. Infrastructure includes the variables by which Nigerian states differ most, and consequently it explains most of the variation in the business environment among states.

Knowing that infrastructure and, to a lesser extent, inputs and institutions are the main impediments to a more friendly business environment in Nigeria does not help policy makers design appropriate interventions. It is important to determine what specific indicators, if improved, would

Figure 3.4   Contribution of Infrastructure, Inputs, and Institutions

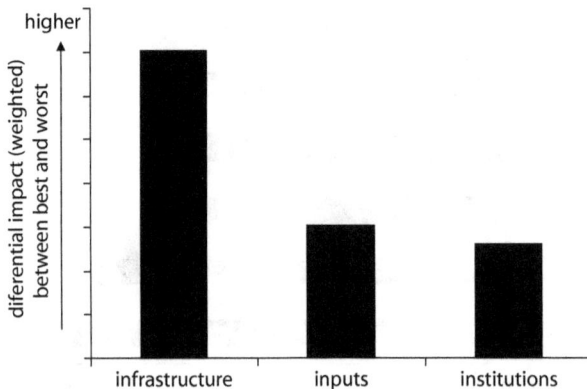

offer the greatest potential to affect the overall business environment as measured by the ICI.

Impact of Reforms

Improving the business environment in Nigeria at the national as well as at the state level remains one of the main challenges of Nigeria's reform program. However the main problem is not to name reforms, but rather to identify which reforms should take priority.

Should all Nigerian states adopt the same reforms? Or should each state identify and implement its own reforms? And what reforms should states implement? Should they reform the indicators in which they perform worst or improve those in which they perform just below average?

We investigate these questions by estimating the impact of different reforms on the ICI. Figure 3.5 shows the impact that reforms would have on the value of ICI in each state if each Nigerian state were to

Figure 3.5   Impact on ICI of Reforming Bottom Three Indicators in Each State

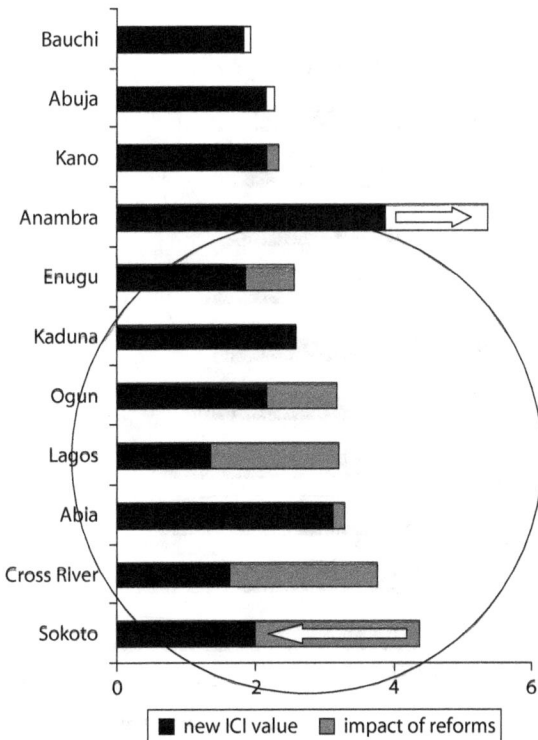

improve its own bottom three indicators.[3] Similarly figure 3.6 shows the resultant impact on the ICI if each state were to reform the three indicators in which each has an average performance. The dark gray bar represents by how much the ICI would improve following such reforms, and the white bar shows by how much the index would deteriorate. The black bar represents the final value of the ICI after the reforms have been implemented.[4]

The results are striking. If only one state-specific reform is adopted it can be seen that some states will benefit more than others. On the other hand, a reform of each state's bottom three indicators will benefit more states in the bottom part of the ranking (figure 3.5), whereas a reform of the middle three indicators will benefit states in the top and bottom part of the ranking, but not those in the middle of the ranking (figure 3.6).

Figure 3.6   Impact on ICI of Reforming Middle Three Indicators in Each State

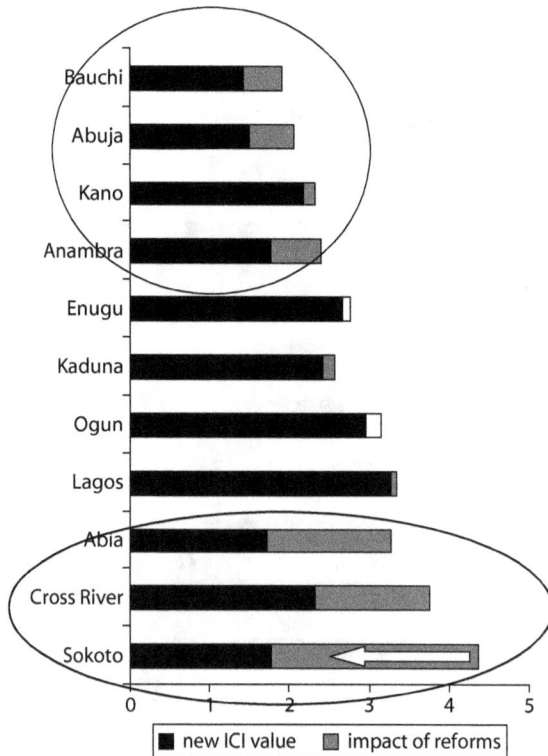

However, if all Nigerian states were to implement the same reforms, will they benefit more than by implementing just state-tailored reforms? We test this hypothesis by identifying and reforming the indicators that are most important in the construction of the ICI. Figure 3.7 clearly shows that although reforms will improve the business climate—shown as a reduction of the ICI—the average impact of additional reforms is lower than the first reform. Hence implementing (the same) additional reforms will not have the same beneficial impact for all states, even if we reform the indicators with the highest weight in the construction of the ICI. On the contrary, some states, for example, Cross River, Lagos, and Abuja, would be better off with only one reform rather than with three identical reforms. Furthermore, because each state has different bottlenecks, by applying the same reforms across the country some states will benefit more than others.

The last test we perform is that of a combination of federal reforms together with state-tailored reforms. More specifically, we estimated the impact on the ICI of one federal reform—improving the cost of finance—with two additional state-level reforms. Figure 3.8 clearly shows that after the value of the ICI is estimated for each possible state-level reform in addition to the national reform (cost of finance), all states benefit from these reforms and that the difference in the quality of the investment climate across states is much smaller. Table 3.1 reports the list of reforms each state should apply to maximize the value of ICI.

This leads us to conclude that reforms in Nigeria will achieve the maximum impact only if state-tailored reforms are accompanied by national reforms.

Figure 3.7   Average Impact on ICI of the Same One or the Same Three Reforms in Each State

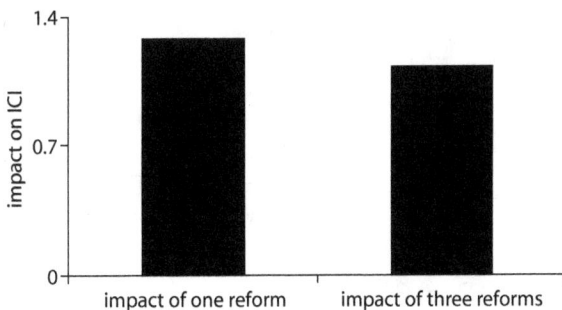

Figure 3.8   Combined Effect of One Federal Reform and Two State-Specific Reforms on ICI

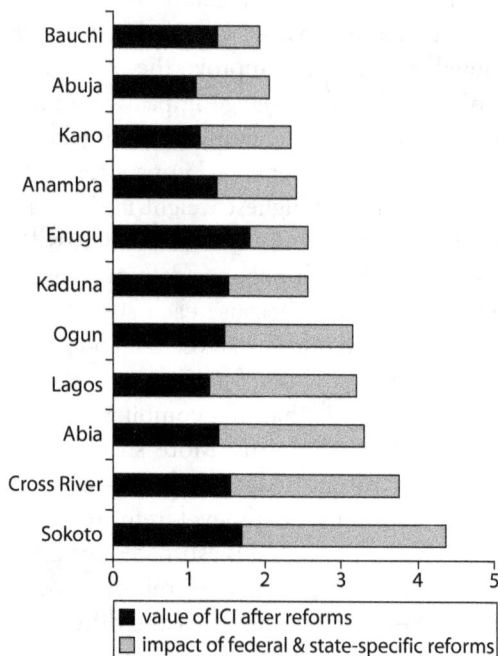

Table 3.1   Three Most Important State Reforms to Improve the ICI

Abia
1. Cost of short-term finance
2. Transport
3. Access to land

Anambra
1. Cost of short-term finance
2. Electricity
3. Tan evasion

Cross River
1. Cost of short-term finance
2. Transport
3. Electricity

Kaduna
1. Cost of short-term finance
2. Transport
3. Electricity

Abuja
1. Cost of short-term finance
2. Bribes for government contract
3. Water

Bauchi
1. Transport
2. Electricity
3. Access to land

Enugu
1. Cost of short-term finance
2. Transport
3. Access to land

Kano
1. Cost of short-term finance
2. Access to finance
3. Electricity

(continued)

Table 3.1   Three Most Important State Reforms to Improve the ICI *(Continued)*

Lagos	Ogun
1. Cost of short-term finance	1. Cost of short-term finance
2. Access to finance	2. Access to land
3. Access to land	3. Sales as intermediate products
Solute	
1. Cost of short-term finance	
2. Access to finance	
3. Electricity	

Notes

1. Examples of variables used are power outages, share of firms with generator, trade credit, share of firms with a loan, losses due to theft, tax evasion, costs of regulations. See Appendix 2 for more details.

2. Because the ICI is a linear combination of factors estimated from a sample of the population, the value of each index has a margin of error.

3. Identified as those with the highest weight and the lowest performance across states. In this instance, "reform" is defined as an improvement in a state-level indicator equivalent to the corresponding value of the best state.

4. If the reform deteriorates the ICI, then the sum of the black and white bars represent the value of the index after the reforms.

CHAPTER 4

Access to Finance

Capital is a key input to any business. An efficient financial system that is able to allocate financial resources quickly and cheaply to their most productive uses is an essential part of a sound investment climate. For Nigerian firms, the Investment Climate Survey data and other indicators suggest that finance imposes important constraints on business expansion.

Access to Credit in Nigeria

Access to finance and, to a lesser extent, the cost of finance are perceived by Nigerian firms as the second most important constraint to doing business. This obstacle however does not affect all firms equally. As figure 4.1 shows, the smaller the firm, the bigger the problem in access to finance and in the cost of finance.

Domestic firms complain about access to finance twice as much (53 percent) as do foreign firms (25 percent), which often have access to their own external financing. Similarly small firms complain more often (59 percent) than do medium (35 percent) and large firms (11 percent). Access to finance seems to be more of a problem in less industrialized states (60 percent) compared with more industrialized states (49 percent).

Figure 4.1   Access to and Cost of Finance in Nigeria

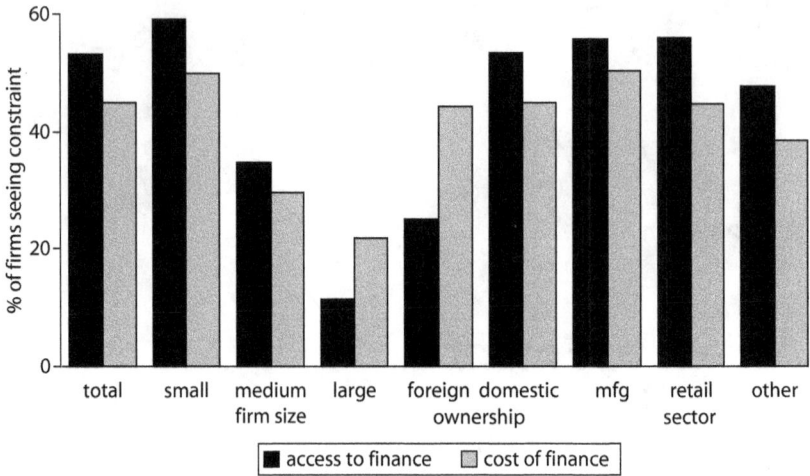

Source: ICA Survey.

Across states there is equally a significant variation of perceptions in regard to cost of finance. For example in Bauchi, 77 percent of firms perceive it as a major constraint compared with Sokoto at 20 percent.

In international benchmarking only Brazil has a worse perception of access and cost of finance (61 percent and 83 percent, respectively). Business owners in all other comparator countries are markedly less likely to cite finance as an obstacle (figure 4.2).

Objective indicators seem to confirm these perceptions. Nigerian entrepreneurs rely predominantly on their own internal funds and retained earnings (70 percent) as well as purchases on credit from suppliers and advances from customers (25 percent). Only a very small proportion of businesses owners borrow money from their family and friends (4 percent). It is striking that the formal financial sector, banks and other financial institutions, is used for only 1 percent of Nigerian businesses' financial needs (figure 4.3).

As one would expect, larger firms do tend to borrow more from the formal sector, but even the largest firms rely heavily on retained earnings rather than seeking bank financing. Only 2 percent of medium and large firms choose to borrowing from banks, and less than 1 percent of smaller firms do so. Interestingly larger firms also rely more heavily on supplier credit and advances from customers at 35 percent compared to the 25 percent of smaller firms (see table 4.1). This might reflect the increased

Figure 4.2   Firms' Perceptions of the Financial Sector Obstacles—International Comparison

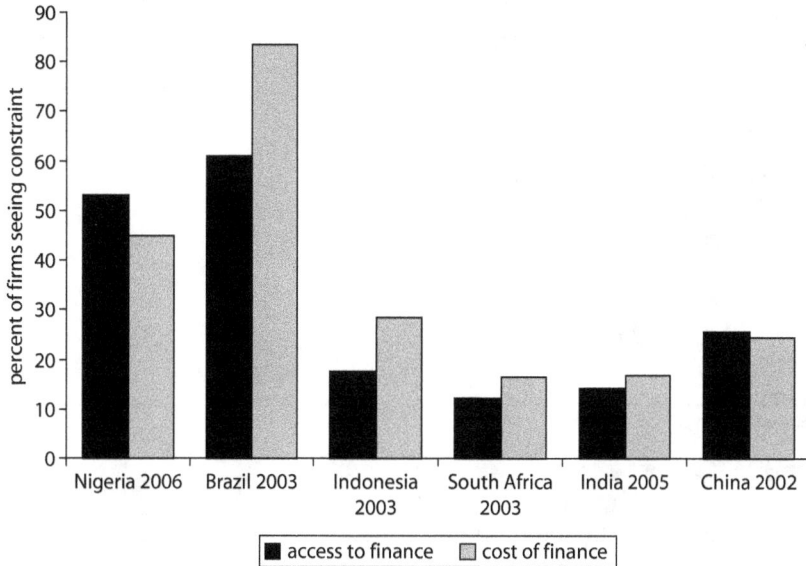

Source: ICA Survey.

Figure 4.3   Sources of Credit for Nigerian Businesses

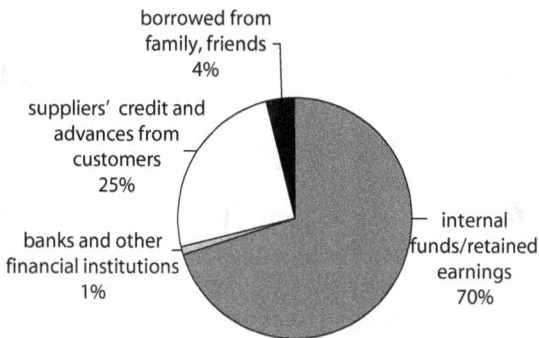

Source: ICA Survey 2008.

market power of larger firms, which can be used to coerce their smaller suppliers and customers into financing their cash flow requirements.

The heavy reliance on internal sources of finance is particular to Nigeria. A comparison with other countries puts the Nigerian situation in stark relief. Although only 1 percent of formal sector firms in Nigeria access bank borrowing, the proportion in China is more than a quarter and

Table 4.1   Sources of Short-Term Finance in the Nigerian Formal Sector

Percentage of short-term financing from	Total	Size			Ownership	
		Small	Med.	Large	Dom.	Foreign
Internal funds/ Retained earnings	70	70	71	61	70	69
Borrowed from banks and other financial Institutions	1	1	2	2	1	6
Purchases on credit from suppliers and advances from customers	25	25	25	35	25	23
Borrowed from family, friends and other informal sources	4	4	2	1	4	1

Source: ICA Survey.

in India it is close to one-third (see table 4.2). This means that businesses in those countries do not rely heavily on supplier credit or advances from customers. This improves cash flow in the whole economy and provides a greater incentive to deliver products and services in a timely manner—a key metric in an increasingly competitive global environment.

When it comes to longer-term financing, entrepreneurs in many countries rely on friends, family, angel investors, and venture capitalists willing to risk their own resources to back promising new ventures. These traditional sources of capital are almost nonexistent in Nigeria, in which business owners are forced to rely even more heavily on their own internally generated resources for longer-term financing than they do for short-term financing (see table 4.3). The data indicate that Nigeria's capital markets lack depth. The banking sector is not yet playing an effective role in advancing credit to the private sector, and the venture capital market remains at a very early stage of development.

This is confirmed by other sources of data. An international comparison of domestic credit to the private sector underscores the lack of depth of the Nigerian financial sector (measured by M2/GDP). Dynamic economies such as Malaysia and South Africa are at 117 percent and 78 percent, respectively, whereas Nigeria at 18 percent of GDP remains below the Sub-Saharan Africa average of 30 percent. Intermediation to the private sector (measured by credit to the private

Table 4.2   Sources of Short-Term Financing in the Formal Sector—International Comparison

Percentage of short-term financing from	Nigeria 2008	Brazil 2003	China 2003	India 2005	Indonesia 2003	Kenya 2007	S. Africa 2003
Internal funds/ Retained earnings	70	44	13	47	38	73	66
Borrowed from banks and other financial Institutions	1	30	27	32	16	7	17
Purchases on credit from suppliers and advances from customers	25	15	2	9	4	17	12
Borrowed from family, friends and other informal sources	4	5	8	9	20	3	1
Issued new equity/debt	—	4	12	2	2	—	1

Source: ICA Survey.

Table 4.3   Sources of Long-Term Finance in the Formal Sector—International Comparison

Percentage of long-term financing from	Nigeria	Brazil 2003	China 2003	India 2005	Indonesia 2003	Kenya 2007	S. Africa 2003
Internal funds/ Retained earnings	92	56	15	52	42	77	58
Borrowed from banks and other financial institutions	1	26	21	33	20	15	33
Supplier credit and other informal sources	2	9	1	5	3	4	1
Family/friends and other informal financial sources	4	2	8	8	24	3	1
Issued new equity/debt	0	5	12	2	2	0	0

Source: ICA Survey.

Figure 4.4   Domestic Credit to the Private Sector

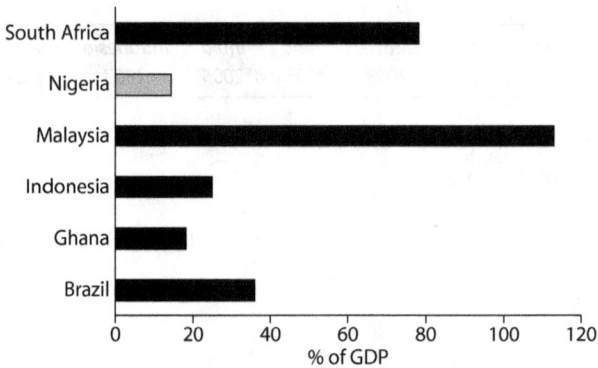

Source: World Development Indicators 2006.

sector/GDP) also remains below peer countries (see figure 4.4). Nigeria's private sector is starved of credit and remains behind not only dynamic Asian economies but also many African competitors.[1] But the situation is starting to improve. Starting from a small base, credit to the private sector is growing at a rapid pace. Between 2003 and 2007 it grew steadily from N1.2 trillion to N4.9 trillion. That represents an increase of more than 400 percent.[2]

Nigerian Banking Practices

In mid-2004, the Central Bank of Nigeria (CBN) requested that all deposit banks raise their minimum capital base from US$15 million to US$192 million by the end of 2005. This process resulted in a reduction in the number of banks in Nigeria, from 89 to just 25. Moreover, in the process of meeting the new capital requirements, banks raised the equivalent of about $3 billion from domestic capital markets and attracted about $652 million of foreign direct investment (FDI) into the Nigerian banking sector.[3]

As a result of this successful consolidation process, the Nigerian banking sector is now well capitalized. With capital adequacy ratios (CARs) at 18.8, the Nigerian banking sector is much more liquid than its peers and surpasses many of the world's most advanced economies (figure 4.5). Meanwhile nonperforming loans (NPLs) have dropped to a manageable 7.7 percent as asset quality continues to improve.

Despite this improved performance, credit to the private sector remains constrained. By looking at formal sector financing in more detail, it can be

Figure 4.5   Capital Adequacy Ratios and Nonperforming Loans—International Comparison

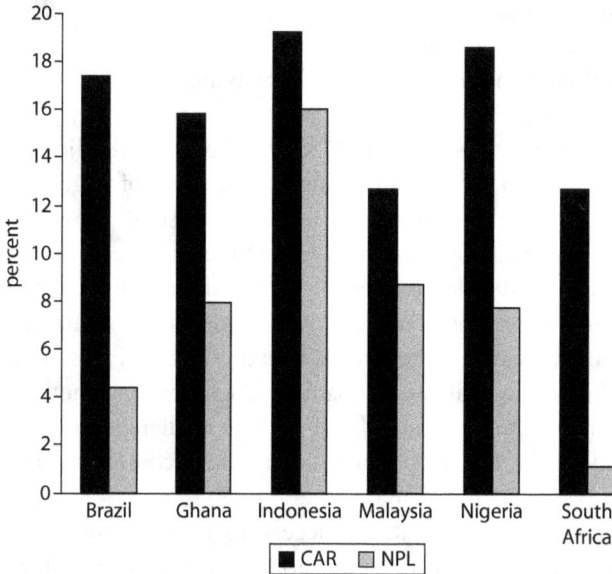

Source: IMF baseline analysis of financial sector, October 2007.

Table 4.4   Access to Credit—International Comparison*

% firms with**	Nigeria	Kenya	Ghana	South Africa	India	China	Brazil
Overdrafts	8	21	13	68	53	25	74
Line of credit or loan	4	25	17	38	36	92	35

Source: ICA Survey.
* For South Africa, India, China, and Brazil "lines of credit" are included in "overdrafts" and not with "loans."
** The weighted average used for Nigeria and Kenya.

seen that only 8 percent of Nigerian firms have an overdraft and only half that amount have access to lines of credit. Without such facilities many firms will experience constrained growth and difficulty in managing their cash flow. As the numbers above also confirm, firms will be forced to rely more heavily on retained earnings and supplier credits.

An international comparison, presented in table 4.4, shows just how little access to credit Nigeria's businesses have. More than two-thirds of South African businesses have an overdraft or line of credit and more than one-third have access to loans. Similar figures are seen in Brazil and India. Even African competitors such as Kenya and Ghana are far ahead of Nigeria in access to formal credit.

Table 4.5 demonstrates that there is very little difference between firms based in Lagos and those elsewhere. Being close to the center of the nation's banking sector does not appear to confer any advantage on Nigerian businesses. As we would expect, the larger the firm, the greater the access it has to such facilities: almost a quarter of large firms have an overdraft compared with less than 6 percent of small firms.

What is also striking is the high rate at which foreign firms located in Nigeria used overdrafts and lines of credit compared with domestic firms. Foreign firms use both facilities about five times more than do domestic firms. It is not clear whether this is because foreign firms are more used to resorting to formal sector banking facilities or whether they are approved more often for such facilities. The challenge for Nigeria is how to expand credit to the private sector while controlling risk through improved banking supervision.

Although the overall rate of access to finance from formal sector sources is low, there is also great variation between industry groupings (figure 4.6). Most of the industry groupings converge around the averages of 7 percent for overdrafts and 4 percent for loans and lines of credit. The exception to this is garment manufacturers. Only 1 percent of them have access to any formal sector sources of credit.

One reason that so few Nigerian firms rely on the banking sector might be the cost and duration of the loans that are available. Average interest rates in the formal sector are 14 percent, and inflation in 2007 was 6.6 percent, according to the Central Bank of Nigeria. Inflation has gradually been brought under control starting from a high in 2003 of 24 percent; it has been in single digits since 2006. This presents borrowers with a high real interest rate (5.6 percent), which might deter them from taking such loans (see below).

Table 4.5   Access to Credit in the Formal Sector

% of firms with	Total	Small	Size Med.	Large	Ownership Dom.	Foreign	Location Outside Lagos	Lagos
Overdrafts	8	6	13	24	8	38	8	7
Lines of credit/loans	4	3	6	15	4	23	4	3

Source: ICA Survey.

Figure 4.6   Access to Credit in the Formal Sector by Industry Grouping

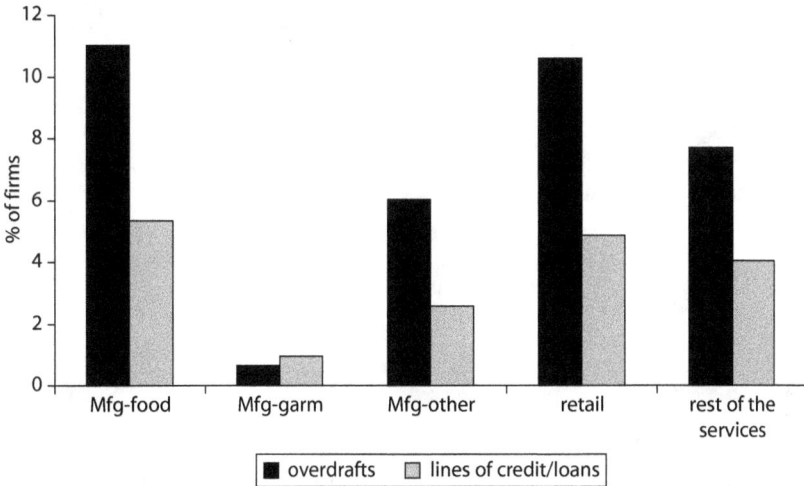

Source: ICA Survey.

Table 4.6   Cost of Debt and Duration—International Comparison

	Nigeria 2008	Brazil 2003	China 2003	India 2005	Indonesia 2003	Kenya 2007	S. Africa 2003
Average annual interest rate	14	22	5	12	14	15	11
Real interest rate (using GDP deflator)	6	11	5	8	9	15	0
Duration (months)	21	42	49	49	23	38	68

Source: ICA Survey and World Development Indicators.

An international comparison reveals that Nigeria is at about the mid-point in regard to bank interest rates (table 4.6). What is different in Nigeria is the duration of the loans. Nigerian entrepreneurs are not able to get loans that exceed two years. Loans in China and India are available for twice as long, and South African entrepreneurs are able to secure loans of almost six years. This allows South African business owners to plan with more certainty and provides them with the financial capacity to overcome short-term challenges in business performance or the broader macroeconomic climate. Developing a facility that provides Nigerian banks with access to longer-term financing would allow them to appropriately match

Table 4.7   Collateral—Formal Sector versus Informal Firms

		Formal	Informal
Percentage of firms whose loans required collateral		79	83
Value of collateral required (percentage of loan)		135	161
Type of collateral required (% of firms with affirmative answers)	Land, buildings	66	40
	Machinery and equipment	23	8
	Accounts receivable and inventories	24	21
	Personal assets of owner (house, etc.)	37	81
	Other	8	0

Source: ICA Survey.

maturities of assets and liabilities and should encourage banks to increase the tenor of their loan portfolio.

Another aspect of cost of finance is collateral requirements. Requiring collateral for loans is a widespread practice in Nigeria. Close to 80 percent of loans to Nigerian enterprises require collateral (table 4.7). The collateral required ranges from 135 percent of the loan value for formal sector firms to 161 percent for informal firms. Loans to formal sector firms most often require land and buildings as collateral, whereas loans to informal firms are more often secured against the personal assets of the owner, usually his or her house. Nigeria's banks have some way to travel to move toward reduced collateral requirements. This nationwide situation is particularly pronounced in the north.

Reasons for Loan Applications and Rejections

Until recently finance appeared to be a scarce commodity in the Nigerian economy. Banks had weak balance sheets, a weak credit culture, and a higher rate of nonperforming loans. Undercapitalized banks charged high spreads to meet the high costs of doing business. To a large extent these issues were resolved during the recent banking consolidation process. With stronger balance sheets, Nigeria's banks are now under more pressure to develop their asset base and search for new and profitable loan markets. Nigeria's bankers complain that there is weak enforcement of corporate governance, accounting, and auditing and a general lack of transparency that results in a lack of trust throughout the whole system, but especially in the small and medium-sized enterprise (SME) sector.

The great majority of Nigerian firms would like increased access to bank financing. More than 70 percent of the firms would apply for a loan. But when they are asked why they do not apply for bank loans, Nigerian entrepreneurs cite burdensome application procedures (21 percent), high interest rates (20 percent) and collateral requirements (20 percent) as the main reasons. (table 4.8)

Beneath this aggregate picture, however, the reasons for not applying for a loan differ greatly by firm size. First, almost 80 percent of small firms would like to have access to banks, whereas only 20 percent of large firms would. Furthermore smaller firms are much more affected by complex loan application procedures (22.9 percent) and unattainable collateral requirements (22.2 percent) than are larger firms (3.3 percent and 5.8 percent). A higher percentage of smaller firms (20 percent compared with 14 percent of large firms) also complain that interest rates are not favorable, a reflection of the fact that banks view smaller firms as more risky and often charge them higher interest rates.

Concrete results of loan applications confirm the perception that collateral requirements and complex loan procedures are the main reasons for a low banking penetration in Nigeria (table 4.9). Close to 55 percent of loan applications from small and micro enterprises are rejected because of unacceptable collateral or cosigner requirements. Surprisingly more

Table 4.8   Reason for Not Applying for Loans—Formal Sector

% of firms citing as main reason for not applying for loans	Small	Medium	Large	Total
No need for a loan—establishment has sufficient capital	22	48	77	28
Application procedures for loans or line of credit are complex	23	15	3	21
Interest rates are not favorable	20	19	14	20
Collateral requirements for loans or line of credit are unattainable	22	11	6	20
Size of loan and maturity are insufficient	1	2	0	1
Did not think it would be approved	10	4	0	9
Other	1	2	0	2

Source: ICA Survey.

Table 4.9   Loan Application/Rejection

		Medium/ large	Micro/ small
	% of firms applying for loans/lines of credit	11	9
	% of rejected applications	53	72
Reasons for rejection of loans/lines of credit	Collateral or co-signers unacceptable	62	55
	Insufficient profitability	8	10
	Problems with credit history/report	—	8
	Incompleteness of loan application	19	12
	Concerns about level of debt already incurred	—	5
	Other	12	11

Source: ICA Survey.

than 19 percent of medium and large firm applications are rejected because of an incomplete loan application, much higher than the rate for small and micro (12 percent). These problems could be resolved by loan officers working closely with business owners before the applications are submitted or on submission to ensure that they are all complete.

How Nigeria's States Differ in Access to Finance

The main pattern of enterprise finance that emerged at the national level, especially the lack of access to formal sources of credit, is replicated at the state level with generally very little variation between states. Approximately two-thirds to three-quarters of enterprises across Nigeria rely on their own internal sources of finance. This ratio does not vary much either by region or by state (table 4.10). Entrepreneurs from Enugu rely most heavily on internal sources (60 percent) and least heavily on family and friends (12.8 percent). Businesses in Sokoto rely most heavily on internal sources and much less heavily on family and friends (1.3 percent).

Borrowing from family and friends drops off dramatically when it is required for longer-term needs. For long-term financing, micro enterprises in many states are 100 percent reliant on their own retained earnings. Cross River is again the only exception in which close to a quarter of businesses are able to rely on supplier credit and customer advances for long-term financing.

Larger firms have slightly more access to formal sources of credit, such as overdrafts and lines of credit. But there is tremendous variation between the states (table 4.11). Bauchi state has the least access to overdrafts and lines of credit for formal sector firms, both at 1.3 percent, whereas Cross

Table 4.10 Sources of Short-Term Finance in the Formal Sector—Nigeria
(by state)

Percentage of short-term financing from	Abia	Abuja	Anambra	Bauchi	Cross River	Enugu	Kaduna	Kano	Lagos	Ogun	Sokoto
Internal funds/retained earnings	64	77	76	73	65	60	65	63	73	77	77
Banks and other financial institutions	2	0	1	0	4	1	3	1	1	1	0
Supplier credit and customer advances	27	18	19	27	26	26	25	35	26	19	21
Family, friends, and other sources	8	5	4	0	5	13	7	1	1	3	1

Source: ICA Survey.

Table 4.11 Access to Credit in the Formal Sector—Nigeria
(by state)

% of firms with	Abia	Abuja	Anambra	Bauchi	Cross River	Enugu	Kaduna	Kano	Lagos	Ogun	Sokoto
Overdrafts	7	11	3	1	12	8	11	7	7	13	3
Lines of credit/loans	3	5	3	1	14	6	4	2	3	3	2

Source: ICA Survey.

Table 4.12 Reason for Not Applying for Loans—Formal Sector
(by state)

Main reason for not applying for loans	Abia	Abuja	Anambra	Bauchi	Cross River	Enugu	Kaduna	Kano	Lagos	Ogun	Sokoto
No need for a loan—establishment has sufficient capital	17	27	18	N/A	30	23	32	30	39	31	20
Complex loan procedures	28	19	23	31	25	15	28	13	16	15	33
Interest rates are not favorable	19	21	29	34	16	27	21	29	16	11	12
Unattainable collateral requirements	25	24	18	29	16	21	15	19	14	27	21

Source: ICA Survey.

River has the highest access, with 13.7 percent of firms having access to lines of credit and 12.0 percent having access to overdrafts.

When the subnational data are analyzed, it is also apparent that business owners in different parts of the country have very different reasons for not applying for a loan. The data indicate that there are large variances in the percentage of firms that apply for loans and lines of credit, ranging from 17 percent in Abia to 39 percent in Lagos (table 4.12). Entrepreneurs from Bauchi who do apply for loans are much more likely to be accepted (75 percent of loan applications are successful) than those from Lagos in which only 12 percent of loan applications are accepted. The only reported reason for rejecting a loan application in Bauchi is incomplete information on the application, whereas in Lagos loans are almost always rejected because of unacceptable collateral. These large regional differences indicate that it will be difficult if not impossible to improve credit to the private sector without combining a federal and a state-by-state approach to this issue.

Notes

1. The average for domestic credit to the private sector in Sub-Saharan Africa is 18 percent of GDP.

2. Banks and the National Economy: Progress, Challenges and the Road Ahead. Presentation by Prof. Soludo, Governor of the Central Bank of Nigeria, February 12, 2008, Abuja Sheraton.

3. Okonjo-Iweala and Osafo-Kwaako, *Nigeria's Economic Reforms: Progress and Challenges*. Brookings Institution Report, 2007.

CHAPTER 5

Entrepreneurship and Managerial Capacity in Nigerian Firms

Productivity improvements—the key element to continued competitiveness—is a function not just of capital and labor, but also of that additional factor of production known as entrepreneurship. To what extent does entrepreneurship provide for productivity improvements in the face of a poor investment climate? And more specifically, to what extent does this happen in Nigeria? Earlier efforts to assess this relationship[1] have used latitudinal data across countries and have isolated non-traditional export firms as the proxy for strong entrepreneurship. These studies suggest that productivity gains—achieved as a result of entrepreneurial innovation[2]—depend on the policy environment. More specifically, in weak or strong policy environments small policy changes can have a significant impact on entrepreneurialism. However, in environments in which the investment climate is neither very weak nor very strong, small policy adjustments evoke a feeble entrepreneurial response. Productivity improvements require more structural, institutional reforms.[3] What is the current relationship between the key variables of investment climate, productivity, and entrepreneurship in Nigeria? How can this line of enquiry be strengthened?

Defining Entrepreneurship

Part of the challenge in investigating these questions is arriving at a sufficiently measurable definition of entrepreneurship. Taking nontraditional export firms as the proxy for good entrepreneurship reflects the fact that these firms tend to be the larger, more profitable, and more technologically advanced. But entrepreneurship is not limited to the tradable sector, let alone the nontraditional segment of this sector. An alternative measure is therefore required to provide a more broadly representative picture of entrepreneurship.

More recent entrepreneurship research[4] was based on a questionnaire comprising 18 questions covering four key areas of entrepreneurship management, namely, operations, monitoring, targets, and incentives. The operations dimension attempts to isolate management effort to streamline and introduce efficiencies into production processes. The monitoring questions focus on the tracking and reviewing of process and individual worker performance and management responsiveness. The targets dimension entails an assessment of the type, realism, and transparency of the targets used by the enterprise. The incentives dimension provides a measure of management approach to bonuses, to promotion, and to dealing with good and poor performers. In summary, the questions provide a set of criteria by which to distinguish between good and bad entrepreneurial management. These questions reflect an approach in line with much of the theory about entrepreneurship as an integrator/coordinator by which resources are deployed and managed to exploit market opportunities through performance-based methodologies and practices. The results, albeit for European and U.S. markets, indicated that "better management practices are significantly associated with higher productivity, profitability, Tobin's Q, sales growth rates and firm survival rates."[5] In addition, higher levels of competition are associated positively with better management practices.

Developing the Management Questionnaire for Nigeria

In adapting this model to the sample base available from the Nigeria survey, some 10 questions covering the four areas—operations, monitoring, targets, and incentives—were posed to 408 manufacturing firms drawn from the overall sample frame. The subsample comprises 135 food, 98 garment, and 175 other businesses. The questions posed are summarized in table 5.1.

Table 5.1   Building the Entrepreneurial Management Practice Index (EMPI)

Category	Question
Operations	1. How do you improve your manufacturing process?
Monitoring	2. How do you track performance?
	3. How do you review your performance indicators?
	4. What happens if there is a part of your firm that is not achieving the agreed results?
Targets	5. What kind of time scale are you looking at with your targets?
	6. How tough are your targets?
Incentives	7. How does your bonus system work?
	8. If you had a worker who could not do his or her job, what would you do?
	9. How do workers get promoted?
	10. If you had a star performer in your staff who wanted to leave, what would you do?

The questions are open ended, and the responses need to be ranked in accordance with criteria that can serve to distinguish between superior and inferior management practices. The following five-level categorization of entrepreneurship is applied with a score of "1" representing poor practice. A score of "3" constitutes some good practice. A score of "5" represents best practice. This scoring approach is henceforth referred to as the entrepreneurial management practice index (EMPI).

Management Practices across Firms

It is illustrative to look first at the frequency distributions of the Nigeria sample. This distribution for Nigeria is set out in figure 5.1.

The first characteristic to notice in figure 5.1 is that the distribution of Nigerian firms is skewed toward the mid to bottom part of the spectrum. There are no firms that score above 4, the "best practice" rating. Second, Nigerian firms show a bipolar distribution: either they are poorly run or they have an average score. Firms are positioned predominately at the end of the range—that runs at about 1.5 to 2—or are slightly above the rating of 3, with the largest number of observations at about 3.5.

There is no significant difference in the EMPI scores by size of firms. Although large firms score marginally higher than small firms, the difference is minimal and hence insignificant. Similarly, the sector breakdown does not suggest significant differences in management practices. However, firms in export-processing zones (whatever the sector) show a higher rating than firms not in the export zones. Similarly firms in the "economic"

Figure 5.1   Frequency Distribution of Nigerian Firm Management Scores

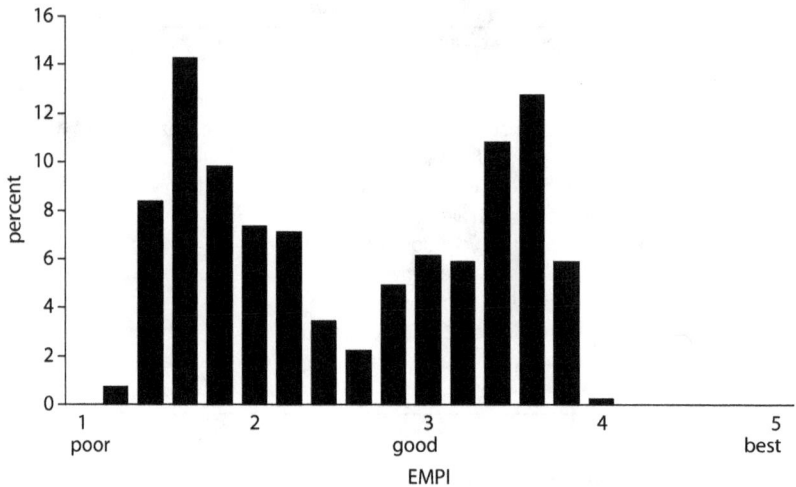

capital of the country, Lagos, show a higher level of entrepreneurship management practice than firms in the rest of the country.

When looking at the level of entrepreneurial ability by location (figure 5.2), we see that only two states perform above average in our EMPI—Lagos and Ogun—with scores well above 3. The other states present a similar score between 2.12 and 2.55.

Apart from size, sector, and location, there are other factors that could influence management performance of firms such as age of the establishment and the experience and education of the firm owner/manager. These determinants were tested by running a multivariate regression and controlling for different firm characteristics (sector, size, location). In the case of age, firms were categorized as new (less than 5 years), young (between 6 and 13 years) and old (more than 13 years). The sample of firms was divided into "good" and "poor" managed firms.[6] Not surprisingly, age does not appear to be a significant determinant of good managerial practice. Old or new firms show the same level of managerial capacity. More experienced managers do tend to run their companies better. However this positive impact on the EMPI score diminishes as the experience level reaches approximately 20 years. The impact on the EMPI was also assessed against the education levels of the owner/manager using the following three-tiered set of education categories: (i) little education (less than secondary completed or no education), (ii) some education (secondary completed and some university), and (iii) high education (graduate or postgraduate

Figure 5.2   Entrepreneurship Management Practice Indicator (EMPI) Results by State

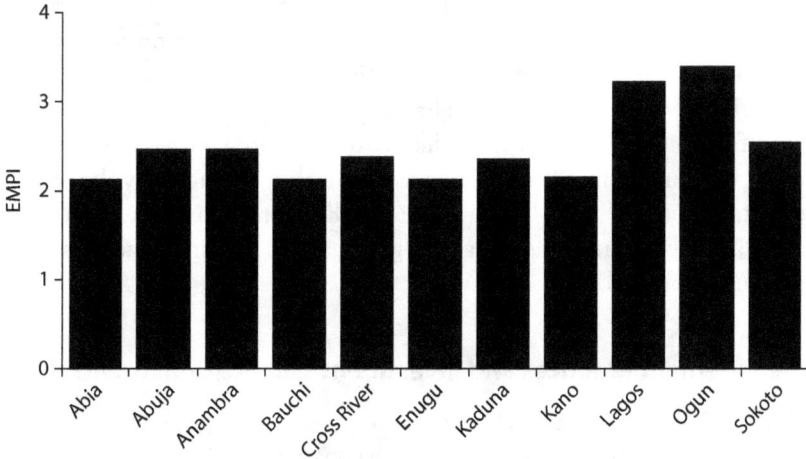

qualification completed). The results were highly significant. Firms with owners having completed a secondary degree are 12 percent more likely to be better managed compared with those with little or no education. Similarly, firms whose managers have a university education are 40 percent more likely to be better managed relative to those with low education.

The relationship between staff training and management practices was also investigated. Do firms that are better managed also provide more training to their staffs? And does staff training improve the way firms are managed? To address the first question, a dummy variable for training was regressed on the EMPI. It indicated that better managed firms are approximately 30 percent more likely to provide training to their staffs. This result is strongly significant even when controlled for a number of firm characteristics. However, the second question was addressed with a focus on the monitoring subcomponent of the EMPI. Because monitoring depends on a great deal of staff participation, it was hypothesized that staff training would improve the ability of staff to better monitor the production process and hence to improve the managerial practice of the establishment. The data tend to confirm the hypothesis. Firms that offer training are approximately 20 percent more likely to have better "monitoring." This correlation is strongly significant. But when we controlled for export status, the correlation becomes insignificant. Although an order of causality cannot be established, it is still observed that better managed firms provide more training and a better trained staff is more responsive to management efforts to introduce effective monitoring practices, especially for export firms.

Finally there is the impact of technology absorption and managerial practice to consider. Are better managed firms also more prone to adopt new technology? The data do indicate that the better managed firms are more likely to adopt foreign technology. More specifically, better managed firms are 30 percent more likely to adopt foreign technology. This result is strongly significant. However this is driven mainly by the export orientation of the firm. If a control is applied for export status, then the correlation becomes insignificant. Once again, an order of causality cannot be established.

Management Practices and Investment Climate Constraints

Table 5.2 provides a summary of how good versus poor "management practice" firms rank investment climate constraints. We can see that even when using this classification the top three constraints identified more generally by firms in Nigeria—power, finance, and transport—are also identified as major problems to both groups of good and poor managed firms. The only notable exceptions where the ranking of obstacles are

Table 5.2   Share of Firms Ranking a Constraint as One of the Top Three by Managerial Performance Level

	Managerial Performance Level (%)	
Constraint	High	Low
Electricity	93	91
Transportation	40	45
Access to Finance	45	44
Access to Land	21	32
Tax Rates	16	24
Finance Cost	20	14
Informal Sector	11	9
Crime, theft and disorder	18	9
Political Instability	5	7
Tax Administration	8	7
License	6	5
Corruption	7	4
Inadequately educated workforce	3	4
Labor Regulations	3	3
Customs and Trade Regulations	4	0
Courts	0	0

significantly different are land and taxes, where low-performing firms complain more than better managed firms. On the contrary crime is the only constraint where better managed firms complain more than poor performers. This confirms what already mentioned in the Business Environment chapter. Crime appears to be a significant constraint to Nigerian firms, especially better managed firms, even more than corruption. This perception is confirmed by objective data on cost of crime. Better managed firms in Nigeria lost double the amount of sales due to theft, robbery, and arson (3.8 percent) compared to 1.8 percent for poorly managed firms.

Implications for Productivity, Firm Performance, and Investment Climate

To what extent do our EMPI measures of better management practice have a similar strong association with firm performance? Correlations of average EMPI against value added per worker generated significant results indicating that better managed firms were able to improve productivity performance (figure 5.3).

More specifically "good management performers" are some 60 percent to 80 percent more productive than "poor performers." This is confirmed both by using value added per worker as well as TFP as measure of firm

Figure 5.3   Value Added per Worker by Managerial Performance

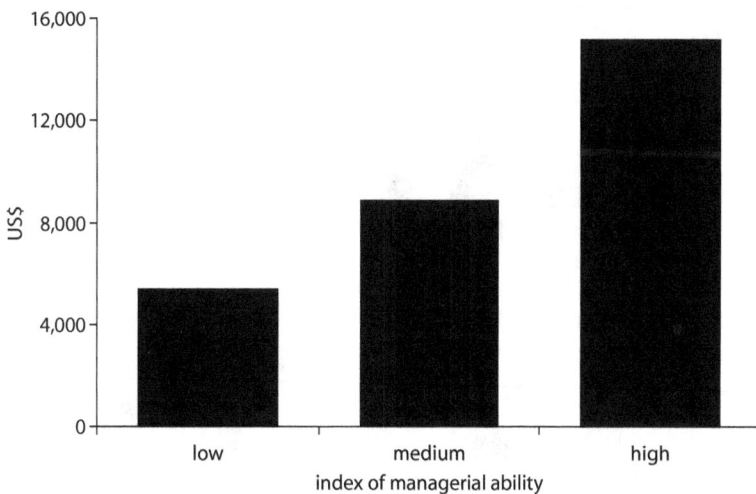

performance. Moreover where management performance was significant, state dummies were not, suggesting that in the majority of states management practices are a more significant determinant of productivity than location. The exception to these results occurred in Lagos and Ogun, where the location dummy remains marginally significant at the 10 percent level. Interpreting this will require some additional analysis, but prima facie, it suggests that these two states have some other economic benefits with a positive impact on productivity performance that is absent in the other states.

To what extent does managerial ability compensate for a bad business climate in Nigeria? Are firms better managed able to increase their productivity even in a poor business environment? This question was investigated by interacting the good/poor managerial practice dummy with a dummy for high- and low-productivity states—constructed using the level of value added per worker. As presented in figure 5.4 our data show that, in states with low productivity, firms better managed are approximately 80 percent more productive compared with firms that are poorly managed. Similarly in states with already high productivity, the better management of firms is able to add an additional 30 percent to 40 percent more productivity.

What do these conclusions imply? The analysis suggests that the more entrepreneurial firms have a greater capacity to exploit opportunities that

Figure 5.4   Productivity Differentials Due to Good Management Performance in Strong and Weak State Environments

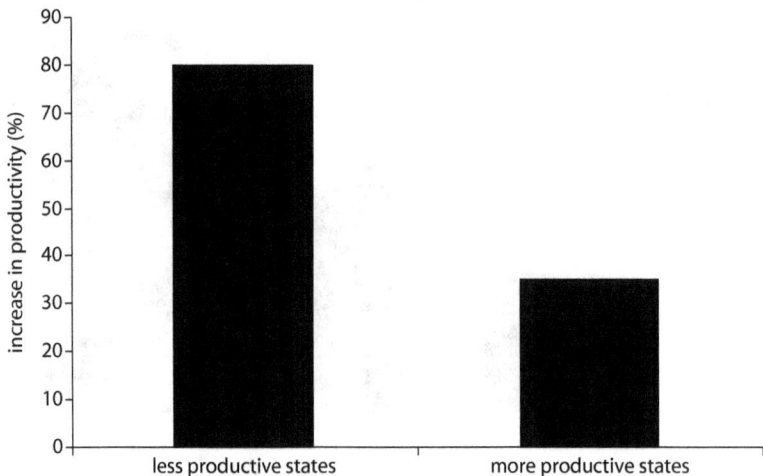

impact productivity performance whether or not investment climate is relatively favorable. At the same time, improving both the investment climate and the managerial ability of firms will ensure the highest impact on enhancing productivity.

Notes

1. M. Iyigun and D. Rodrik; "On Efficacy of Reforms: Policy Tinkering, Institutional Change and Entrepreneurship," March 2004.
2. What the authors refer to as "cost discovery."
3. J. Schumpeter, "Capitalism, Socialism and Democracy," 3rd ed., 1950.
4. By Bloom and Van Reenan from the London School of Economics and Political Science (LSE).
5. N. Bloom and J. Van Reenen, "Measuring and Explaining Management Practices Across Firms and Countries," Centre for Economic Performance (CEP) Discussion Paper #716, March 2006.
6. Firms with EMPI above the mean score of 2.49 are grouped as the "better performers" and those firms with score below this average are consider "poor performers."

CHAPTER 6

Other Aspects of the Investment Climate: Functioning of the Labor Market, Micro Enterprises, and Gender Differences

To what extent are enterprises in Nigeria constrained by labor market regulations and skills availability? Do micro firms or firms managed by female entrepreneurs face different constraints? The Investment Climate Survey can provide some guidance in response to these.

Labor Market

An overwhelming majority of firms in Nigeria do not perceive either a shortage of skilled workers or labor regulations to be a major or very severe impediment to growth. Only about 1 percent of all manufacturing firms report either constraint to be a major or very severe impediment. The same holds true for the retail and services sector.

Labor skills. As table 6.1 shows nearly half of manufacturing firms in Nigeria report that their typical worker has more than 12 years of schooling. This is higher than all the comparator countries. However, for most countries the typical manufacturing sector worker has between 7 and 12 years. In contrast, only 31 percent of Nigerian manufacturing firms have workers with that level of schooling. Relative to its comparators, only

Table 6.1   Percent of Firms Saying That the Average Worker in the Firm Has Completed Different Levels of Schooling

	0–6 years	7–12 years	>12 years
Kenya (2006)	15	68	17
South Africa (2003)	10	78	12
Brazil (2003)	33	59	8
India 2002	26	55	19
Nigeria (2007)	**21**	**31**	**48**

Source: Investment Climate Surveys.
Note: Cross-country comparisons are only for manufacturing enterprises. Comparable data are unavailable for the other comparator countries.

about a fifth of Nigerian firms' typical workers have fewer than six years of schooling.

About 26 percent of firms provide training to their workers. In the firms that provide training, nearly 60 percent of skilled workers and about 23 percent of unskilled workers received training. Among manufacturing firms, a firm that provides training has a value added per worker that is nearly 25 percent higher than firms that do not. However, this effect is driven largely by the size of the firm. Figure 6.1 shows the proportion of firms with on-the-job training and the percentage of workers trained across a range of firm characteristics. There is a modest "firm size–training provision" correlation: firms with 100 plus employees are more than twice as likely to provide training as firms with fewer than 20 workers. Holding other factors constant, only the firm-size correlation is significant. Unlike results from similar analyses in South and East Africa, firms that are active in HIV prevention or testing of their workers appear no more likely to provide training (Ramachandran and others 2005). There was also no evidence for a particular state having a particular effect on training.

Conditional on providing training, firms in Nigeria compare favorably with comparator countries with respect to the proportion of the skilled workforce that is trained. Only Kenya reports a higher proportion. It is important to point out once again, that the data used in table 6.2 are unable to illustrate any differences in the quality of training provided.

Labor regulations. Labor regulations are considered even less of an impediment. Less than 1 percent of all sampled firms find labor regulations to be a major constraint: manufacturing (1.3), retail (0.4), and services (0.1). Just over 2 percent of firms reported that labor regulations had affected hiring or firing decisions. This is consistent with other

Figure 6.1   Percent of Firms Providing Training and Percent Workers Trained

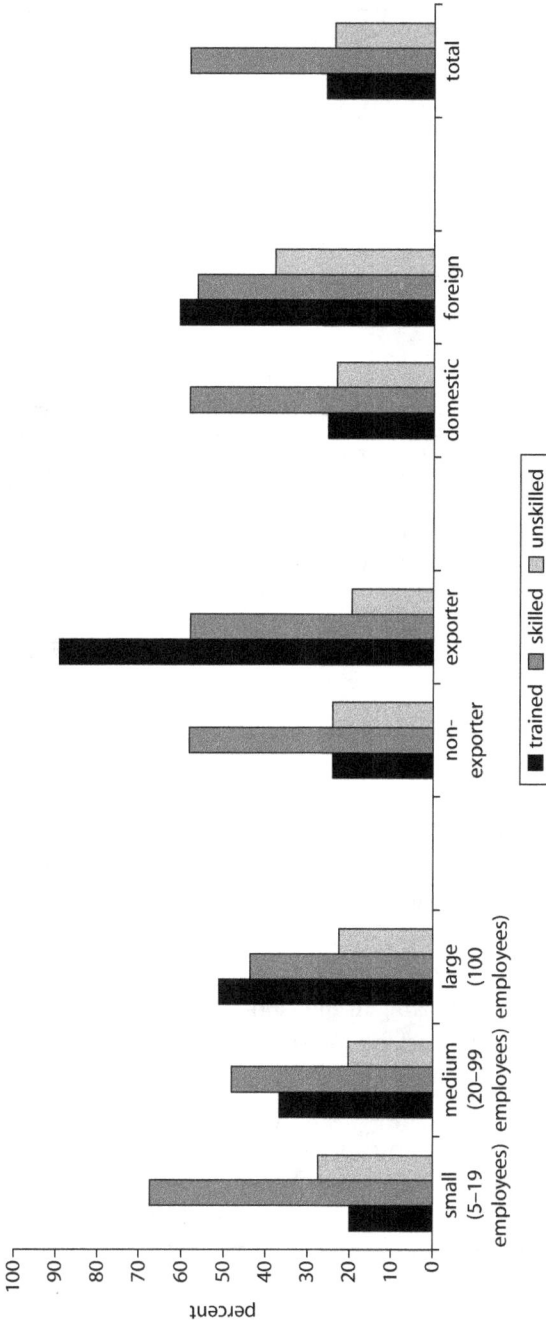

legend: trained, skilled, unskilled

y-axis: percent

x-axis categories: small (5–19 employees), medium (20–99 employees), large (100 employees), non-exporter, exporter, domestic, foreign, total

Source: Investment Climate Surveys.

Note: The figure shows percentage of firms that provide firm-based training and the percentage of skilled and unskilled workers that are trained. Only data for manufacturing firms are available.

Table 6.2   Firm-Based Training: Prevalence and Percent of Workers Trained

Country	% firms offer training	% production workers trained	% nonproduction workers trained
India 2005	16	7	6
Indonesia 2003	23	—	—
Kenya 2006	41	66	50
Venezuela 2006	49	—	—
Nigeria 2006	**26**	**58**	**24**
South Africa 2003	64	45	47
China 2003	72	48	25

Source: Investment Climate Surveys.
Note: Cross-country comparisons are only for manufacturing enterprises.

Table 6.3   Median Monthly Wages by Occupation in 2005 U.S. Dollars

Firm Category	Production workers	Nonproduction workers
<20	70	86
20–99	91	109
>99	120	179
Domestic	77	98
Foreign	151	116
Total	78	98

Note: All wages are converted to 2005 dollars using the exchange rate from the World Development Indicators.

evidence. The Doing Business report collects detailed information on how labor regulations affect hiring, firing, and rigidity of employment. On the basis of these regulations, the report calculates measures of labor regulation. Nigeria is ranked in the top one-third of all countries with respect to labor regulations. This ranking is considerably higher than that of all other comparators.

Wage comparisons across firms in Nigeria. Understanding the wage-setting mechanisms operating in the labor market is vital to the design of policies to improve the performance of the labor market. Table 6.3 shows tentative evidence that very large firms pay wages for production workers that are nearly 70 percent higher than firms with fewer than 20 employees. The same is true of nonproduction worker remuneration which is twice as much in large firms relative to smaller firms.

The location of a firm exerts an important effect on compensation. Consistent with the literature on agglomeration, firms located in the more industrialized states pay nearly 35 percent more for production workers and 49 percent more for nonproduction workers than firms in the less industrialized states.

Micro Firms

Constraints to business. Table 6.4 indicates that the main obstacles faced by micro firms[1] are the same as those faced by firms in the formal sector:[2] electricity, access to finance, and cost of finance followed by corruption, transportation, and crime.

There is a significant variation in these results across states (table 6.5). For instance, 92 percent of firms in Anambra perceive electricity to be a significant constraint, whereas in Ogun, Sokoto, and Cross River about 60 percent of firms do. The variation across states is higher when we look at some of the other main constraints: 79 percent of firms in Abia perceive access to finance as a significant constraint, compared with only 20 percent of firms in Sokoto; 73 percent of firms in Abia and Anambra perceive the cost of finance to be a significant constraint, versus only 13 percent of firms in Sokoto; and no firms in Sokoto identify corruption as a major problem, whereas it is ranked as significant by 77 percent in Bauchi. As for transportation, it is reported to be a significant constraint by 14 percent of firms in Kaduna and by 53 percent of firms in Bauchi.

The impact of some of these constraints on micro firms' costs is similar to that seen in the formal economy. The breakdown of indirect costs amounts to approximately 12 percent of total sales (table 6.6). Electricity (7.5 percent of sales) and production lost while in transit (2 percent of sales) are the two main drivers of such costs. These affect different types of firms in different ways. Electricity is more of a problem for manufacturing micro firms (8 percent). As for the production lost while in transit, which represents a loss of 2.1 percent of sales, it affects registered firms in particular (2.8 percent versus 1.5 percent) and firms located in the less industrialized states (3.1 percent of sales versus 1.1 percent). Bribes represent a loss of 1.4 percent of sales. Finally, theft, robbery, and arson are responsible for a loss of 1.1 percent of sales, varying according to the level of industrialization (1.4 percent in the less industrialized states versus 0.7 percent in the remaining).

Comparison between formal sector and micro firms. As we can see from figure 6.2 and figure 6.3, there are minor differences between firms in the formal sector and micro firms in the identification of their main constraints and in regard to indirect costs.

Micro firms and firms in the formal sector are equally affected by power outages (table 6.7). The most significant difference is that more firms in the formal sector have generators (86 percent versus 53 percent of micro firms).

Table 6.4 Major or Very Severe Constraints as Reported by Micro Firms

Constraint	TOTAL	Registered		Industry			State		State	
		Yes	No	Manuf.	Retail	Other	More industrialized	Less industrialized	Better regulatory environment	Worse regulatory environment
Electricity	72%	68%	75%	82%	68%	80%	66%	78%	72%	71%
Access to finance (e.g., collateral)	64%	66%	62%	66%	63%	69%	61%	67%	58%	70%
Cost of finance (e.g., interest rates)	56%	58%	54%	59%	54%	60%	52%	60%	50%	60%
Corruption	35%	39%	33%	35%	35%	40%	34%	38%	36%	35%
Transportation	33%	32%	33%	41%	32%	24%	30%	35%	31%	34%
Crime, theft, and disorder	32%	35%	29%	39%	30%	36%	29%	35%	26%	37%
Tax rates	25%	33%	18%	36%	24%	18%	25%	26%	22%	28%
Access to land for expansion / relocation	24%	22%	26%	27%	23%	25%	25%	23%	24%	24%
Macroeconomic environment	20%	25%	15%	25%	18%	22%	23%	16%	22%	18%
Tax administration	19%	26%	13%	29%	17%	18%	19%	20%	19%	19%
Business licensing and permits	14%	14%	14%	17%	14%	4%	14%	14%	11%	17%
Political environment	14%	16%	12%	11%	14%	13%	14%	13%	16%	12%
Practices of competitors in informal sector	14%	20%	9%	14%	14%	18%	17%	11%	16%	12%
Customs and trade regulations	8%	10%	7%	5%	10%	2%	11%	5%	7%	9%
Inadequately educated workforce	5%	6%	4%	4%	5%	7%	7%	3%	4%	6%
Telecommunications	4%	6%	3%	6%	4%	4%	4%	5%	5%	3%
Labor regulations	2%	2%	3%	2%	2%	4%	3%	2%	4%	1%

Source: Investment climate survey in Nigeria.

Table 6.5 Major or Very Severe Constraints as Reported by Micro Firms—by State

Constraint	TOTAL	State										
		Abia	Abuja	Anambra	Bauchi	Cross River	Enugu	Kaduna	Kano	Lagos	Ogun	Sokoto
Electricity	72	79	64	92	83	61	80	62	75	68	58	60
Access to finance (e.g., collateral)	64	79	68	71	63	76	60	48	65	73	52	20
Cost of finance (e.g., interest rates)	56	73	56	73	57	67	44	46	62	59	32	13
Corruption	35	29	28	25	77	43	40	14	43	43	32	0
Transportation	33	29	32	35	53	22	48	14	24	46	36	20
Crime, theft, and disorder	32	42	16	35	13	33	54	24	24	41	32	0
Tax rates	25	23	12	21	30	43	18	20	29	32	22	13
Access to land for expansion/ relocation	24	17	20	27	30	31	18	24	31	25	20	0
Macroeconomic environment	20	8	44	8	3	29	28	20	22	25	16	7
Tax administration	19	19	16	17	20	39	8	16	32	14	10	13
Business licensing and permits	14	10	4	15	0	16	24	2	16	21	20	7
Political environment	14	10	20	6	27	18	12	18	13	19	4	0
Practices of competitors in informal sector	14	2	28	21	0	12	20	10	25	14	10	0
Customs and trade regulations	8	0	24	6	3	8	2	4	7	19	8	13
Inadequately educated workforce	5	0	12	0	0	4	10	0	3	16	8	0
Telecommunications	4	2	0	2	7	6	8	4	4	5	2	0
Labor regulations	2	2	20	2	0	0	4	0	4	0	0	0

Source: Investment climate survey in Nigeria.

Table 6.6   Indirect Costs—Micro Firms

Indirect costs as % sales	TOTAL	Registered		Industry			State	
		Yes	No	Manuf.	Retail	Other	More in industrialized	Less indus- trialized
Electricity	7.5	8.2	6.9	8.4	7.1	9.5	7.8	7.2
Production lost while in transit	2.1	2.5	1.5	1.8	2.1	2.5	1.1	3.1
Bribes	1.4	1.7	1.2	1.7	1.3	1.3	1.1	1.7
Theft, robbery, or arson	1.1	1.1	1.0	1.2	1.0	0.9	0.7	1.4
Total indirect costs	12.1	13.8	10.5	13.1	11.5	14.2	10.8	13.5

Source: Investment climate survey in Nigeria.

Figure 6.2   Percentage of Firms Reporting Major or Very Severe Constraints — Formal Sector versus Micro Firms

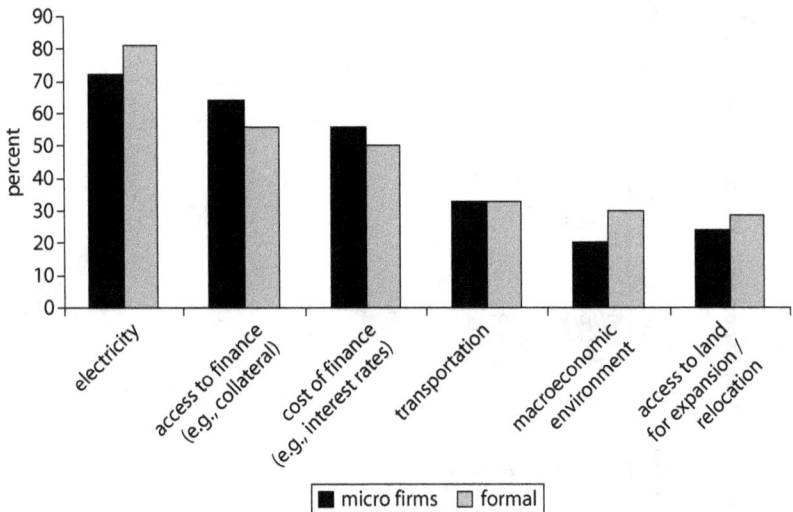

Source: Investment climate survey in Nigeria.

On Regulatory Burden

Not surprisingly, firms from the formal sector also face a heavier regulatory burden. They spend a higher percentage of senior management time with regulations, and they have a higher probability of being visited by officials. Table 6.8 shows that, on average, 4.5 percent of senior management time of micro firms is spent with government regulations. Obviously this burden falls more heavily on registered firms. State/local government-level regulation appears to be slightly more of a burden than

Figure 6.3   Indirect Costs—Formal Sector versus Micro Firms

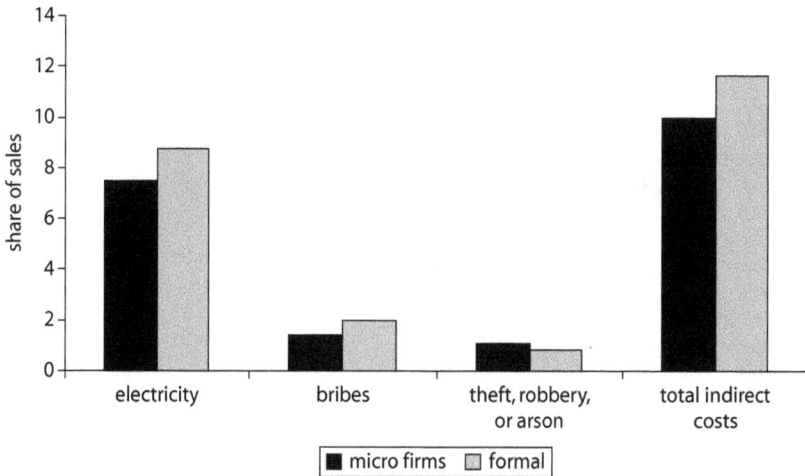

Source: Investment climate survey in Nigeria.

Table 6.7   Infrastructure Perceptions—Formal Sector versus Micro Firms

	Quality measure	Formal	Micro
Electricity	% firms experienced power outages	96	98
	Average duration of outages per month (hours)	196	207
	% firms with own generator	66	53
	% electricity coming from own generator	61	60

Source: Investment climate survey in Nigeria.

federal-level regulation. Even though the cost associated with regulations, as a percentage of annual sales, is relatively stable across states, it reaches its maximum in Enugu (4.7 percent of sales) and its minimum in Sokoto (0.8 percent). It is higher for registered firms and for those located in states with a better regulatory environment. On average close to 77 percent of all firms were visited by officials, and on average this occurred 3.8 times each year. The probability of having been visited is higher for registered firms. This probability also varies across states, ranging from 44 percent in Enugu to 93.8 percent in Abia. The number of visits per year is higher for registered firms.

The percentage of annual sales spent on gifts/informal payments, as well as the percentage of the contract value paid, are higher for firms in the formal sector (table 6.9). However, government officials are held in higher regard in the formal sector, where 43.5 percent of firms believe them to have a consistent and predictable interpretation of the law, compared with 32.5 percent of micro firms.

Table 6.8   Regulatory Burden—Micro Firms

Quality measure	TOTAL	Registered		Industry			State	
		Yes	No	Manuf.	Retail	Other	More indus- trialized	Less industri- alized
% senior management time spent with regulations	**4.5**	**5.4**	**3.6**	**4.0**	**4.3**	**6.1**	**4.1**	**5.0**
at the state/local government level	**2.7**	3.3	2.2	2.5	2.6	3.6	2.4	3.1
at the federal level	**1.8**	2.1	1.4	1.5	1.7	2.5	1.7	1.9
Cost associated with regulations (% annual sales)	**2.3**	**3.0**	**1.8**	**2.5**	**2.1**	**3.6**	**2.1**	**2.7**
at the state/local government level	**1.4**	1.7	1.2	1.3	1.4	1.8	1.1	1.8
at the federal level	**0.9**	1.3	0.6	1.2	0.7	1.8	1.0	0.9
% firms visited by officials	**77**	86.2	69.1	77.1	77.2	75.6	76.6	77.5
Number of inspection visits (last 12 months)	**3.8**	4.2	3.3	3.5	3.9	3.4	3.5	4.2

Source: Investment climate survey in Nigeria.

Table 6.9   Perception of Government and Regulations—Formal Sector versus Micro Firms

% firms that agree with statement	Formal	Micro
Consistent and predictable interpretation of the law	43.5	32.5
Informal payments/gifts commonplace	33.2	30.0
Advance knowledge of informal payment/gift	24.6	20.0
Percentage of annual sales spent on informal payments/gifts	2.0	1.4
Percentage of contract value paid to secure contract	5.3	4.3

Source: Investment climate survey in Nigeria.

On average, micro firms identify the difficulty of getting information on what needs to be done to register a business as the most significant obstacle, followed by the time needed to complete registration procedures (38 percent and 33 percent, respectively). The financial cost of completing registration is a lesser burden (table 6.10). On average, only

Table 6.10   Percentage of Firms Reporting Major or Very Severe Obstacles to Registering a Business—Micro Firms

							State	
		Registered		Industry			Better regulatory environment	Worse regulatory environment
Obstacle	TOTAL	Yes	No	Manuf.	Retail	Other		
Difficulty of getting information on what you need to do to register	**38%**	34%	41%	37%	38%	33%	45%	31%
Time to complete registration procedures	**33%**	24%	40%	33%	23%	38%	42%	24%
Financial cost of completing registration	**30%**	27%	34%	29%	31%	31%	39%	22%
Minimum capital requirements for registered enterprises	**25%**	21%	28%	24%	24%	31%	30%	20%
Financial burden of taxes on registered enterprises	**19%**	18%	19%	17%	20%	13%	24%	14%
Administrative burden of complying with all tax laws	**15%**	7%	22%	13%	15%	16%	16%	15%
Other administrative burdens imposed on registered businesses	**15%**	10%	18%	14%	16%	7%	17%	12%
Strict labor market rules registered businesses must comply with	**12%**	13%	11%	12%	12%	11%	16%	8%

Source: Investment climate survey in Nigeria.

30 percent of micro firms complain about registration costs. An even lower percentage identify the minimal capital requirements for registration (25 percent) and the financial burden of taxes on registered enterprises (19 percent) as the most significant obstacle.

Women Entrepreneurs in Nigeria

National levels of participation. In Nigeria, about 20 percent of formal enterprises are run by women—14 percent of all manufacturing firms and 26 percent of firms operating in the services sector. As such, Nigeria does not rank high in comparison with other African countries, as figure 6.4 shows. The share of women entrepreneurs is higher in Nigeria than in Niger, Mauritius, DRC, and Mauritania, but it is lower than in Madagascar, Angola, Uganda, and Cameroon, not to mention Botswana and Cape Verde.

   Sector characteristics. A fundamental difference between men and women entrepreneurs exists in the type of sector in which they operate. Women operating in the formal sector are highly concentrated in a few specific activities—mostly retail (23 percent) and the garment industry (37 percent). Men are more evenly distributed across industrial sectors. Women are almost absent from sectors such as wood, metal, chemicals, construction, and transport, areas in which men dominate.

Figure 6.4   Share of Female-Owned Enterprises in Selected African Countries

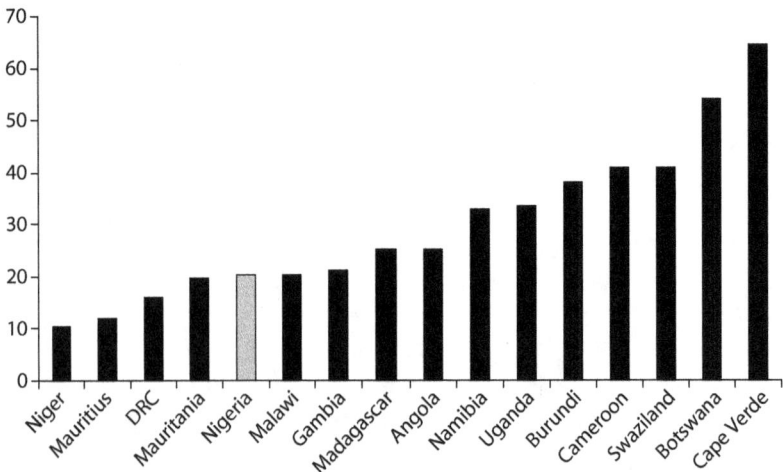

Source: Enterprise Survey data. Only most recent data are included (2005 to 2007). The samples include manufacturing and services sectors.

Regional variations. The level of female participation in entrepreneur-ship varies widely across regions of Nigeria (table 6.11). The states that are part of the southeast region (Abia, Anambra, Enugu), which is tradition-ally a region of traders rather than farmers, as well as the capital state of Abuja and Nigeria's biggest city, Lagos, are all characterized by high rates of female entrepreneurship in the formal sector—in manufacturing, serv-ices, or both. At the other extreme, Bauchi, in the northeast, is the state with the lowest share of formal businesses run by women (manufacturing and services combined). Low rates of female entrepreneurship are also found in the north central states, such as Kaduna and Kano. Table 6.12 provides more sub-sector detail. It shows the percentage of female entre-preneurs in the garment industry and retail by state, it is evident that in the northern states, the percentage of entrepreneurs operating in the garment industry who are women is lower than the national average, at 7 percent in Sokoto, 13 percent in Kaduna, and 17 percent in Bauchi. Similarly, the percentage of women entrepreneurs in retail in the northern states tends to be lower than the national average.

Table 6.11   Percentage of Formal Firms Owned by Women, by State and Sector

	Region*	Manufacturing	Services	Formal (manufac-turing and services)	Micro
Sokoto	NC	9.0	24.7	21.0	35.7
Kaduna	NC	9.7	21.6	15.9	49.0
Kano	NC	12.8	19.4	15.9	23.9
Bauchi	NE	10.3	16.2	13.5	17.2
Abuja	MB	14.1	42.9	30.8	36.4
Lagos	SW	14.1	25.5	20.1	25.0
Ogun	SW	15.3	23.1	19.7	50.0
Cross River	SS	13.4	20.6	18.2	20.4
Anambra	SE	12.0	25.9	21.1	22.9
Enugu	SE	22.2	27.9	25.9	30.6
Abia	SE	21.7	23.7	22.9	18.8
All		13.8	24.7	20.2	29.5
More industrialized states[†]		13.3	25.3	19.7	35.5
Less industrialized states		15.0	24.0	21.0	23.2
Number of observations		898	900	1,798	485

Source: Investment climate survey in Nigeria.
Note: The sample does not include public and foreign-owned enterprises. Percentages in *italics* calculated for samples with less than 30 obs. States are ordered according to their north-south location.
* NC: north central; NE: northeast; MB: midbelt; SW: southwest; SS: south south; SE: southeast.
[†] More industrialized states are Lagos, Abuja, Kano, Kaduna, Ogun.

Table 6.12   Percentage of Female Entrepreneurs by State and Selected Subsectors

State	Garment	Retail
Sokoto	7.1	17.6
Kaduna	12.5	13.9
Kano	31.3	18.9
Bauchi	16.7	10.5
Abuja	33.3	28.6
Lagos	53.8	37.7
Ogun	66.7	29.0
Cross River	30.0	22.9
Anambra	60.0	20.0
Enugu	64.0	18.6
Abia	40.0	14.8
All Nigeria	37.3	23.1

Source: Investment climate survey in Nigeria.

However, as table 6.11 portrays, female entrepreneurship is not systematically higher in more or less industrialized regions (20 percent versus 21 percent). The micro enterprise sector is different. At 30 percent, the rate of female entrepreneurship is higher than it is in the formal sector and rates of female entrepreneurship in the micro sector are higher in more industrialized states (36 percent versus 23 percent).

Age and education levels. Male and female entrepreneurs operating in the formal sector do not differ much with respect to their personal traits, such as age and education. Women are only slightly younger than men, and there are no remarkable differences in education (see table 6.13). In the micro sector, although the education level is lower than in the formal sector for both men and women, women have a higher education level than men. Although 31 percent of men do not go beyond the primary education level in the micro sector, this percentage is only 21 percent among women, with a higher share of women in this sector with vocational training. Moreover, unlike for men, the percentage of women with a graduate degree is as high in the micro sector as in the formal sector.

Gender Differences in Investment Climate Constraints

Figure 6.5 shows the percentage of male and women entrepreneurs who believe that a constraint is "major" or "very severe," for the formal sector (manufacturing and services combined)[3] and the micro sector. In the formal sector, men and women tend to agree on the level of severity of many constraints. Electricity, access to finance, and cost of finance

Table 6.13   Education Level of the Business Owner, by Industrial Sector

	Formal (manufacturing and services)		Micro	
	Male-owned	Female-owned	Male-owned	Female-owned
Up to primary	13.3	14.4	30.8	20.9
High school	42.7	41.6	48.8	48.5
Vocational	37.0	40.5	18.7	27.6
Graduate degree	7.0	3.5	1.8	3.0
Total	100.0	100.0	100.0	100.0

Figure 6.5   Percentage of Entrepreneurs Who Declare That a Specific Constraint Is "Major" or "Very Severe"

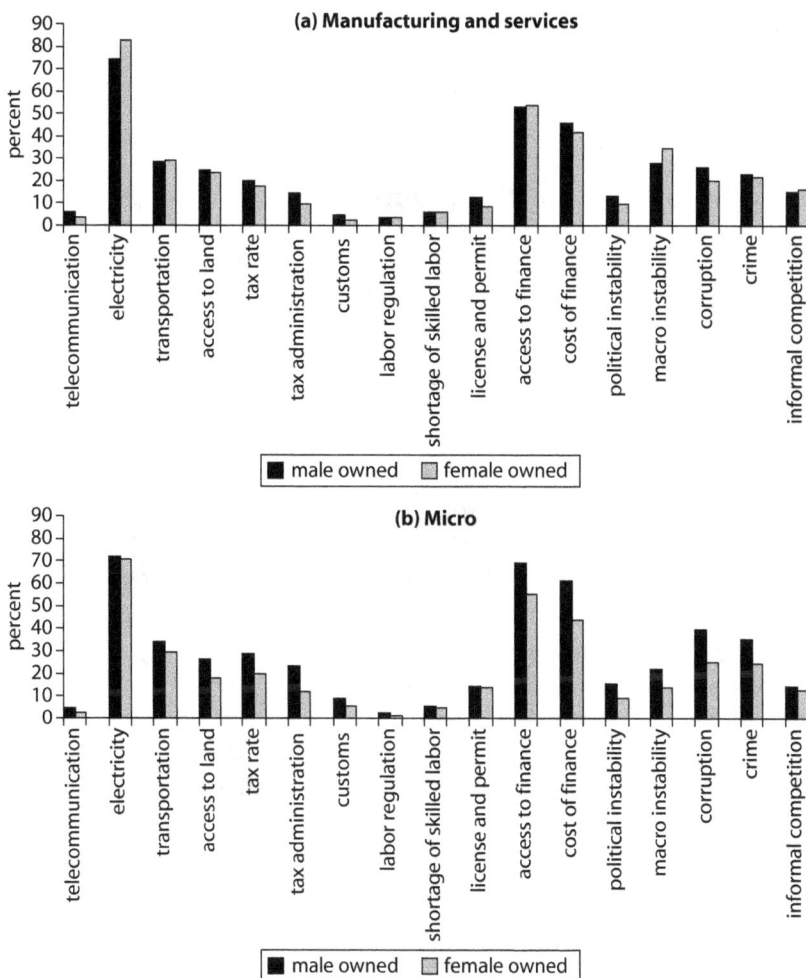

stand out as the three most severe constraints for both men and women. In the micro sector, the most severe constraints are the same as in the formal sector—electricity, access to finance, and cost of finance. Moreover, corruption and crime are relatively more important than in the formal sector, and this is true for both men and women.

The results presented in figure 6.5, although giving a summary picture of the differences in perceived constraints by gender of the business owner, do not take into account that women and men entrepreneurs are not all the same—as noted, they operate in different industrial sectors and have different personal characteristics. This can affect their opinions about the severity of the obstacles they face. Controlling for these variables, the gender gap in the formal sector is usually small in percentage points. The gender gap in perceptions (adjusted for individual and firm-level characteristics) is very different in the micro sector.

In the micro sector men judge almost all constraints as more severe than women do, and the gender gap for several constraints is larger than in the formal sector. The biggest differences exist for corruption, crime, and cost of finance (10 or more percentage points difference), but substantial gaps are also found for tax administration, access to finance, access to land, and macro and political instability.

Because perceptions could be misleading, in what follows we provide some evidence of the difference between men and women business owners in "objective" measures of the quality of the business environment, focusing on those constraints that in the opinion of the entrepreneurs are the most pressing ones—electricity, access to finance, and cost of finance.

Electricity. Both men and women are extremely likely to have experienced a power outage. Ownership of a generator is similar for men and women in manufacturing, whereas in the micro sector the percentage of female entrepreneurs owning a generator is much lower (45 percent vs. 56 percent). Although women operating in manufacturing experienced on average 10 hours a month longer (or +4 percent) power outages than did men in the same sector, they do not appear to have been more affected by those power outages in regard to average percentage of sales lost (table 6.14). However, in the garment subsector, in which a large percentage of female entrepreneurs operate, women do indeed claim larger losses than men because of power outages (10.7 percent vs. 8.2 percent of sales, on average). In looking at retail—which is another "female-intensive" sector— there are differences depending on whether this activity is formal or informal (micro). In the formal retail sector women appear to have experienced lower losses, whereas in the informal, micro sector women experienced larger losses than men as a consequence of power outages.

Table 6.14   Percent of 2006 Sales Lost as a Consequence of Power Outages, by Industrial Sector and Sex of the Business Owner

	Male	Female
Manufacturing	10.1	9.4
Services	8.9	7.2
Micro	8.6	8.6
Selected industrial sectors:		
Garment industry	8.2	10.7
Retail (formal sector)	8.6	6.4
Retail (micro sector)	8.1	8.6

Source: Investment climate survey in Nigeria.

Table 6.15   Composition of Working Capital, by Sector and Sex of Business Owner

	Manufacturing		Services		Micro	
	Male	Female	Male	Female	Male	Female
Internal funds	66.9	65.6	72.3	76.4	75.7	76.0
Purchases on credit/advances						
from customers	28.9	30.8	22.4	18.7	19.6	19.3
Borrowed from:						
private commercial banks	0.8	0.1	1.2	0.7	0.6	0.2
state-owned banks	0.1	0.0	0.0	0.0	0.0	0.0
nonbank institutions	0.1	0.0	0.0	0.0	0.0	0.0
family and friends	2.9	3.3	3.6	3.7	3.7	4.4
informal sources	0.4	0.2	0.4	0.4	0.4	0.1
Other	0.0	0.0	0.1	0.0	0.0	0.0
Total	100.0	100.0	100.0	100.0	100.0	100.0

Source: Investment climate survey in Nigeria.

Access to finance. Men and women rely largely on internal funds and retained earnings for operating capital (66 percent–67 percent in manufacturing, 72 percent–76 percent in services, 76 percent in the micro sector) as well as credit from suppliers and using advance payments from customers (about 30 percent in manufacturing and about 20 percent in services and the micro sector) (see table 6.15). An extremely small minority uses the formal financial sector (less than 1 percent), and only 9 percent of men and 8 percent of women in the manufacturing and service sector applied for a loan in 2006.

For long-term finance, there is again very little difference between men and women (see table 6.16). Both rely almost exclusively on internal funds and retained earnings in manufacturing, services, and the micro sector. The only small difference is that women are more likely in manufacturing and the micro sector to rely on family, friends, and informal networks.

Table 6.16   Purchase of Fixed Assets and Sources of Long-Term Financing, by Sector and Gender

	Manufacturing		Services		Micro	
	Male	Female	Male	Female	Male	Female
% purchasing fixed assets	47.3	45.5	40.9	32.3	24.9	15.4
Sources of financing						
Internal funds	91.6	90.3	93.0	93.9	94.4	88.2
Purchases on credit/advances from customers	2.6	2.5	1.8	1.8	3.5	5.5
Borrowed from:						
private commercial banks	0.7	0.6	1.1	1.4	0.0	0.0
state-owned banks	0.3	0.0	0.1	0.3	0.1	0.0
nonbank institutions	0.2	0.0	0.1	0.0	0.0	0.0
family and friends	4.1	5.9	3.0	2.4	2.0	5.5
informal sources	0.3	0.3	0.5	0.3	0.0	0.9
Issued new equity	0.2	0.2	0.0	0.0	0.0	0.0
Issued new debt	0.0	0.1	0.0	0.0	0.0	0.0
Other	0.0	0.0	0.4	0.0	0.0	0.0
Total	100.0	100.0	100.0	100.0	100.0	100.0

Source: Investment climate survey in Nigeria.

Table 6.17   Percentage of Entrepreneurs with Overdraft and Line of Credit, by Sector and Sex of the Business Owner

	Manufacturing		Services		Micro	
	Male	Female	Male	Female	Male	Female
Overdraft	5.9	4.2	8.5	8.3	5.6	0.7
Line of credit	2.6	2.8	4.0	3.8	4.1	1.4

Source: Investment climate survey in Nigeria.

The evidence also indicates that the percentages of men and women with an overdraft or line of credit are extremely small (see table 6.17), with little differences in the formal manufacturing and services sectors. However, in the micro sector, women are much less likely than men to have overdrafts (eight times less) and lines of credit (about three times less). For those who considered access to finance to be a very serious problem, men were equally divided across three main reasons—high interest rates, lack of collateral, and complex application procedures. Conversely, women were far more likely to blame the complexity of the application procedures (about 35 percent vs. 26 percent of men). Women are also more likely to indicate that they did not believe the loan would have been approved when they decided not to apply for it.

Gender Differences in Productivity

In those activities in which women's participation levels are high, there are no substantial differences between the performance of female-owned and male-owned enterprises. Figure 6.6 shows the ratio of the value added per worker in male-owned over female-owned enterprises. In food and retail this ratio ranges between 0.9 and 1; in garments it is more than 1.2, that is, female-owned enterprises have on average a 20 percent higher value added per worker than male-owned enterprises. This suggests that female-owned enterprises are no less efficient than male-owned enterprises. Women may be capital constrained, but it affects the selection of the type of activity, not the productivity of the firm once the business has been set up.

To verify this, total factor productivities in manufacturing are also esti-mated, using one-step Cobb-Douglas production functions.[4] The results further confirm that there are no significant differences in productivity between male- and female-owned manufacturing enterprises. But that is not the case at the state level. In three states (Bauchi, Kano, and Sokoto) female-owned enterprises are significantly and substantially less produc-tive than male-owned enterprises.

Summary

This chapter has analyzed a range of other variables affecting firm performance and investment climate differences. Clearly labor market

Figure 6.6   Male-Owned to Female-Owned Enterprise Ratio of Value Added per Worker, by Industrial Sector

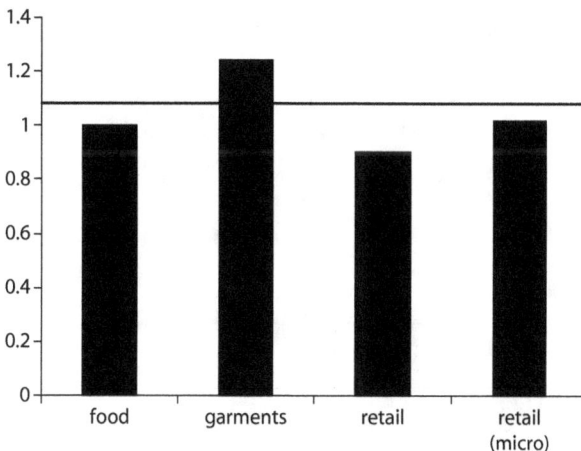

Source: Investment climate survey in Nigeria.

regulations are a minor issue relative to other investment climate constraints. The results for labor skills merit further analysis—looking in more depth at the sector and industry context. The similarities in the ranking of constraints between informal and formal firms and "lack of information" constraints to registration provide important insights for prioritizing reform agendas and designing implementation arrangements. The most relevant differences between men and women entrepreneurs in Nigeria are threefold: (i) propensity to become entrepreneurs, given that only 2 of 10 entrepreneurs are women; (ii) the regional differentials between the southern and northern regions and the concentration of women in specific sectors—essentially garments and retail (in both the formal and micro sectors); and (iii) although women may have greater hurdles entering into business, they do at least as well as men once the enterprise is established.

Notes

1. Micro firms are firms with fewer than five full-time employees.
2. Formal sector consists of small, medium, and large firms.
3. The differences between manufacturing and services in the levels and the gender gap of the business constraints are very small, so we pooled the two sectors in the descriptive analysis.
4. With the logarithm of the value added as the dependent variable as a function of labor (logarithm of the number of permanent employees) and capital (logarithm of the book value of assets).

CHAPTER 7

Conclusions—Framing a Policy Response

This report identifies key obstacles to productivity and competitiveness in Nigeria, based on a survey analysis of some 2,400 firms conducted in 2007 in 11 states. The analysis shows that fostering competition, improving the business environment, and enhancing managerial ability have the potential to generate important productivity gains in Nigeria. Furthermore there is clear evidence that states differ markedly in regard to their business environment and firm performance. This suggests that federal policies and programs to foster new productivity gains will have the maximum impact only if complemented by state-level reforms.

Perception and objective indicators confirm that electricity, finance, and transportation are the three most important investment climate impediments affecting firms across Nigeria.

Power. Virtually all firms in Nigeria experience power outages, and 85 percent of them own a generator. The typical Nigerian firm loses about 10 percent of sales per year to power outages. And unlike other obstacles that affect only some regions or firm sizes, the lack of power affects all firms.

The delivery of additional power and more reliable power is a principal policy objective of the government. Feasibility considerations—including the interlinked need for significant new investment and the challenge of coordinating policy from the gas sector through to the distribution of power—will inhibit the extent to which results can be realized over the short term. This raises the question as to what private sector development results can be pursued during the shorter term as the power sector reforms take effect.

Access to finance. Nigeria's businesses are starved of capital. Although 80 percent of firms would like to have a loan, only 5 percent actually have one. Small firms are particularly affected. Only 20 percent of small firms that did not apply for a loan said that they did not need credit. And when firms in Nigeria do manage to obtain a loan, they get the shortest time to repay it of any comparator countries. The complexity of the application process and the onerous collateral requirements are the main reasons for such low banking penetration.

Finance for enterprise development—particularly micro, small, and medium-size enterprises—remains a high priority under President Yar'Adua's Seven Point Plan and the NEEDS II strategy objectives for private sector development. The commercial bank consolidation exercise and the Central Bank microfinance policy have laid the foundations for new initiatives to deepen and broaden enterprise access to finance. As portrayed in the analysis, there has been a notable deepening in recent years but from a low base. Some banks are increasing their SME lending, and de novo microfinance institutions are entering the market. There are prospects to accelerate this trend during the shorter to medium term, particularly if key FSS 2020 initiatives such as credit bureau and secured financing reforms proceed as scheduled.

Transport. Transport is the third most important constraint accounting for 4 percent of annual sales losses. As more than two-thirds of all Nigerian inputs are delivered by road, the quality of the network is a key issue for the whole economy. Similarly, the efficiency of customs clearances is also a critical factor in transport efficiency. In Nigeria it takes 46 days to clear imports, the second highest among comparator countries. Of all comparator countries, Nigeria remains the most expensive location from which to ship imports or exports—it costs $1,730 to ship a 40-foot container for export and $2,450 to ship for import.

New federal roads investments are planned by the government. Reforms are under consideration for the railways sector, and building on the concessioning of the Apapa port terminals, additional trade facilitation investments, both institutional and infrastructural, would be needed to improve customs clearance performance and port efficiencies. Key feasibility considerations need to be reviewed to determine what transport constraints to private sector development can be addressed over the short and medium term.

Management capacity. Nigerian firms that are better managed are 60 percent to 80 percent more productive than firms that are not. Good managers can be almost as productive in a poor business environment as poor managers are in a good environment. The message is clear: enterprise-level capacity building can result in significant productivity improvements, particularly in already better performing environments. In the best environments, firms with better managers achieve an additional 30 percent to 40 percent increase in productivity over those with poor managers.

In regions with a more dynamic business environment populated by more entrepreneurial and management-efficient firms, more specific technical input in support of key technology or business innovations relevant to specific value chain operations are probably optimal. In the case of environments in which there is weaker entrepreneurship, initial enterprise support is probably best targeted toward broader-based training in, for example, management practice and financial management training.

State governments have asserted their commitment to skills development, but policy statements need to be matched by substantial action. In some states, training and skills development is integrated in their SEEDS action plans, but there is little evidence that policy statements have been matched by action and impact.

States such as Cross River are home to a plethora of vocational institutions and experience high university entrance rates. Despite this, many firms complain about a local shortage of adequate skills, requiring them to search for these skills in the other states. Government and the private sector should work together toward integrating technical skills development into education sector reforms to improve general education levels but also to revamp the quality of vocational training.

Although several private sector associations prioritize capacity building of their membership, there is little capacity in the organizations themselves to deliver training, monitor performance, and measure impact in their reference industry. Firms also need to increase their investment in skills development.

Federal- and state-level reforms. What is the role of federal and state governments in reforming the business environment? The report shows that, because each state has a different business environment, the same federal reforms will benefit some states more than others. Consequently, to maximize the benefit of reforms on the business environment states must complement the national reforms on energy, finance, and transport with state-specific reforms. The study goes on to identify which three reforms would have the biggest impact in each state. Abia, Bauchi, Enugu, Lagos, and Ogun should implement reforms on access to land. Abuja should address issues of corruption and improve access to water. Ogun state should improve vertical integration across firms, and Anambra should improve tax administration.

Next Steps

What are the next steps? Two key initiatives include (i) stakeholder consultations on the diagnostic work contained in this report as well as others and (ii) policy assessment and design.

Stakeholder consultations on the diagnostic work. Every effort has been made to ensure that this diagnostic work meets the highest standards of objectivity and consistency and has the richness required to satisfy the Nigerian call for "evidence-based" policy making. There is a huge potential to use this robust enterprise data set to inform policy and program decisions and provide a benchmark against which to measure the outcomes and impact of these decisions. But this can be achieved only through consultation and dialogue among the key stakeholders, including federal, state, and also municipal governments. Equally important is maintaining a strong dialogue and partnership with the private sector.

Policy assessment and design. Determining that something is important does not mean that it can, or should, be done. In deciding on a policy or program package, decision makers need to take a number of factors into account. A mix of "technical" and "practical" knowledge is required that takes into account considerations of relevance, feasibility, sustainability, and synergies/impact (box 1).

This Investment Climate Assessment provides data that can most substantially contribute to the "relevance" and "measurement" aspects of the policy assessment process. But much more needs to go into good policy design, and that must come from the stakeholders who implement and act on the policies. Detailed design work and the clarification of implementation arrangements must be completed for a policy to become operational. In other words, reform champions will need to be in place, institutional roles and responsibilities agreed on, work plans (with activities, timelines, and targets) established, and budgets made available.

Box 1

Assessing Reform Options

Criteria	Variable	Description of variable
Relevance	Policy priority	Do the actions focus on improvements that can have a measurable impact in support of a key policy or strategic objectives?
Feasibility	Political will and institutional capacity Sequencing	• Does the political commitment for the policy exist? • Beyond the reform champions, is there sufficient institutional capability to implement? • Are there sequencing considerations? Do certain measures better suit shorter- or longer-term time frames?
Sustainability/ cost	Budget and other resource implications	• Are there significant upfront or recurrent cost or revenue gain/loss considerations? • Is the reform financially sustainable? • Can gaps in institutional capacities essential for success be addressed in parallel with implementing the reform program?
Synergies and impact	Demonstration Linkages Measurement	Do the planned initiatives have the potential to catalyze a broader alliance for reform to follow through or scale up? Three elements by which to assess this are as follows: (i) **demonstration effects:** Does the initiative offer quick wins and tangible impacts etc. to lock in commitment and maintain momentum? (ii) **linkages** to other stakeholders and capacity to *scale up reforms* or positive *spillovers* to other areas (e.g., where institutions created for one reform can—based on know-how gained—apply expertise and champion-related orother reforms). Then there are *knock-on effects* where a reform initiative raises awareness and appetite to deal with related reform areas. (iii) **measurement:** Can the policy impact be credibly measured? Do objective and broadly accepted benchmarks exist?

References

Bloom, N., and J. Van Reenen, "Measuring and Explaining Management Practices Across Firms and Countries,", Centre for Economic Performance (CEP) Discussion Paper #716, March 2006.

Eifert, Benn, Alan Gelb, and Vijaya Ramachandran. 2008. The Cost of Doing Business in Africa. Evidence from Enterprise Survey Data. Word Development (forthcoming).

Escribano, A., and J. L. Guasch. 2005. "Assessing the Impact of the Investment Climate on Productivity Using Firm-Level Data: Methodology and the Cases of Guatemala, Honduras, and Nicaragua." Discussion Paper WPS3621. The World Bank, Washington, D.C.

Iarossi et al. 2007. "Business Climate, Productivity and Competitiveness in Armenia: 2002–2005." *Armenian Journal of Public Policy* 2 (2): 153–91.

Iyigun, M., and D. Rodrik. 2004. "On the Efficacy of Reforms: Policy Tinkering, Institutional Change and Entrepreneurship." Unpublished, available at http://ksghome.harvard.edu/~drodrik/INSTDISC.09.27.04.pdf

Kendrick, J. W. 1961. *"Productivity Trends in the United States."* New York: Princeton University Press for the National Bureau of Economic Research.

Lipsey, R. G., and K. Carlaw. 2001. "What Does Total Factor Productivity Measure?" Study paper, Jan. 18. Simon Fraser University, Vancouver, Canada.

Okonjo-Iweala, N., and P. Osafo-Kwaako. 2007. "Nigeria's Economic Reforms: Progress and Challenges." Brookings Institution, Washington, D.C.

Olley, G. S., and A. Pakes. 1996. "The Dynamics of Productivity in the Telecommunications Equipment Industry." *Econometrica* 64 (6): 1263–97.

Ramachandran, V., M. K. Shah, and G. Turner. 2005. "HIV/AIDS and the Private Sector in Africa: Evidence from the Investment Climate Survey Data." World Bank, Washington, D.C.

Schumpeter, J. 1950. *Capitalism, Socialism and Democracy*, 3rd ed. Harper & Row, New York, N.Y.

Soderbom, M., and F. Teal. 2002. *"The Performance of Nigerian Manufacturing Firms: Report on the Nigerian Manufacturing Enterprises Survey 2001."* Prepared for UNIDO and Centre for the Study of African Economies, Oxford University, Oxford.

Solow, R. M. 1957. "Technical Change and the Aggregate Production Function." *Review of Economics and Statistics* 39 (August): 312–20.

Soludo, C. 2008. "Banks and the National Economy: Progress, Challenges and the Road Ahead." Presentation by C. Soludo, Governor of the Central Bank of Nigeria. Abuja Sheraton, February 12, 2008.

Subramanian, U., W. P. Anderson, and K. Lee. 2005. *"Measuring the Impact of the Investment Climate on Total Factor Productivity: The Cases of China and Brazil."* Working Paper WPS3792. World Bank, Washington, D.C.

Transparency International. 2007. Transparency International's Corruption Perceptions Index. Transparency International, Berlin, Germany.

van Wijnbergen, S. 2002. *An Assessment of the Private Sector in Nigeria—A Pilot Investment Climate Assessment.* World Bank, Washington, D.C.

World Bank. 2002. An Assessment of the Private Sector in Nigeria. World Bank. Washington, D.C.

_____. 2006. World Development Indicators. World Bank, Washington, D.C.

_____. Various years. Governance Indicators. World Bank. Washington D.C. (www.worldbank.org/wbi/governance)

Sample Composition

The World Bank's 2007 Investment Climate survey for Nigeria was administered to 2,387 firms in 10 states plus the federal territory. The selection method followed was stratified simple random sampling for the formal economy and simple random sampling for the informal sector. Weights were estimated and used in the analysis where appropriate.[1] Of the total sample, 1,891 were sampled in the formal economy, and 496 in the informal economy. Within the formal economy 50 percent were manufacturing firms and the other half were services. Appendix table 1 shows the sample distribution across states and sectors. Within manufacturing, food (30 percent), garments (23 percent), and other manufacturing (45 percent) represent individual strata. Outside the manufacturing sector, the retail sector accounts for 42 percent of the services, with 58 percent of the firms belonging to the rest of services (**"residual"**) (Appendix table 1).

This sample structure reflects an overall population of approximately 7,500 formal firms and more than 750,000 informal establishments. More than 40 percent of the formal population is in manufacturing (Appendix table 2).

In geographic distribution, Lagos State has the highest number of firms (17 percent), followed by Kano and Ogun State (11 percent). This is not surprising because although Lagos has been and still remains Nigeria's

Appendix Table 1   Distribution of Nigerian Firms by Sector and State

Stratum	Abia	Anambra	Abuja	Bauchi	Cross River	Enugu	Kaduna	Kano	Lagos	Ogun	Sokoto	Total
Food	8	15	22	27	30	16	29	32	40	54	29	302
Garment	20	10	21	19	10	25	26	33	26	19	14	223
Other manufg.	32	34	30	18	30	30	48	47	99	42	13	423
Total manufg.	60	59	73	64	70	71	103	112	165	115	56	948
Retail	28	37	30	20	39	44	37	40	70	32	18	395
Residual	61	45	36	20	62	57	45	40	105	60	17	548
Total formal	149	141	139	104	171	172	185	192	340	207	91	1891
Micro	48	48	25	30	49	50	50	68	63	50	15	496
Total	197	189	164	134	220	222	235	260	403	257	106	2,387

Source: World Bank, Investment Climate Survey in Nigeria.

Appendix Table 2   Population by Sector and Location

Stratum	Abia	Anambra	Abuja	Bauchi	Cross River	Enugu	Kaduna	Kano	Lagos	Ogun	Sokoto	Total
Food	9	39	55	40	70	32	102	130	150	102	77	806
Garment	60	19	48	41	15	58	88	70	80	60	54	593
Other manufg.	63	70	87	70	47	112	211	326	500	200	61	1,747
Total manufg.	132	128	190	151	132	202	401	526	730	362	192	3,146
Retail	84	90	115	88	110	172	179	229	350	158	250	1,825
Residual	125	140	162	87	180	210	221	225	500	300	354	2,504
Total formal	341	358	467	326	422	584	801	980	1580	820	796	7475
Micro	12,000	11,000	1,300	2,290	7,720	10,020	12,880	35,300	649,360	15,077	6,596	763,543
Total	12,341	11,358	1,767	2,616	8,142	10,604	13,681	36,280	650,940	15,897	7,392	771,018

commercial city, Kano is the commercial hub of Nigeria's north and the most populous state in Nigeria, according to 2006 census results.

Most (nearly 60 percent) Nigerian firms in the sample are small enterprises with 5–19 employees. Medium firms, with 20–99 employees, account for 17 percent of the sample, and large firms, employing 100 or more people, constitute less than 2 percent. Finally micro firms, employing fewer than 5 people, represent 20 percent of the sample.[2]

Total Factor Productivity

Productivity measures, such as value added per worker, capital per employee, and unit labor cost are important tools for analyzing firm performance, but these are partial indicators of productivity. Indeed, recent studies have preferred to use much broader measures of productivity. One such measure of overall productivity is total factor productivity (TFP), which despite the divergent views on its concept and measurement, has been widely used in empirical studies of productivity. The traditional approaches to TFP, which date back to the works of Solow (1957) and Kendrick (1961), combine Cobb-Douglas-type production function with the growth accounting method. A distinction is often made between growth in TFP and absolute index of TFP. Although the former, often associated with time series studies, is calculated by subtracting the effect of growth in total inputs from growth in output,[3] the latter (absolute TFP) is represented by the residual (error term) in the Cobb-Douglas production function associated with cross-section studies.[4] However, the interpretation of the residuals as TFP should be done with caution because factors other than technical efficiency could have an effect on the nature and magnitude of the residuals. According to Subramanian, Anderson, and Lee (2005), firm-level variations in TFP may account for a substantial component of the residual values from a regression equation of a production function.

In the present study, we used the production function technique to estimate TFP for manufacturing firms in Nigeria and comparator countries. For each firm, we used value added as output in the regression equation, and the number of employees and book value of assets as measures of labor and capital, respectively. We also included an indicator for Managerial Ability as an additional explanatory variable in the production function. Dummy variables to control for sectors and states were introduced into the equation, so too were interaction terms between capital/labor and the state and sector dummies.

Appendix Table 3   Regression Results of Production Function Estimation

Independent variables	Estimated coefficient	t-statistic
Log(K/L)	0.227***	5.03
Dummy food	−0.212	1.06
Managerial indicator	0.273**	2.07
Abia	−2.054***	3.94
Abuja	−1.179**	2.46
Anambra	−1.852***	3.08
Bauchi	−1.576***	3.13
Enugu	−1.253**	2.30
Kaduna	−1.141**	2.35
Kano	−1.474***	2.92
Lagos	−0.205	0.37
Ogun	−0.507	1.00
Sokoto	−0.876*	1.77
Dummy–Exports	−1.600	1.41
Age	0.027	1.46
Dummy–Medium–Size	−2.065***	3.13
Dummy–Large–Size	−0.164	0.15
Constant	10.625***	3.13
R-squared 0.528		
No. of observations 145		

Note: *, **, *** denote significance at the 10 percent, 5 percent, and 1 percent levels, respectively; all *t*-ratios are in absolute values.

Different variations of the model were estimated, but the results presented in table 2.5 give the best statistical fit in regard to the explanatory power of the model and the significance of the estimated coefficients. The model was estimated by the ordinary least squares method using a robust heteroscedastic correction procedure to take into account heteroscedasticity, which is a common phenomenon in cross-section regressions. We also tested the functional form of the model in regard to omitted variable bias using the Ramsey Regression Specification Error Test (RESET) diagnostic. Results from the RESET find no supporting evidence of omitted variable bias.[5]

We also applied a "blocked *F*-test" technique to test whether the coefficients on state dummies are statistically different or not. The calculated *F*-statistic from this approach is 2.1, with a probability value of 0.0382, implying that the coefficients on the state dummies are statistically different from each other at the 5 percent level.[6]

Total Factor Productivity and Employment

Given that both labor and TFP constitute important components of the production function directly (in the case of labor) and indirectly (TFP) through Cobb-Douglas technology that is disembodied in factor inputs, a link between labor and TFP can be established through the conditional labor demand function. But the effect of an improvement in TFP on labor demand would depend on the nature and extent of "returns to scale" in the production function. It is expected that under constant returns to scale, a percentage change in TFP would lead to a proportionate change in labor demand. In the case of increasing returns to scale and decreasing returns to scale, however, an increase in TFP would lead to smaller and larger changes, respectively, in labor demand.

Applying the proposition above to the Nigerian data yields the estimated conditional labor demand equation in Appendix table 4. All estimated coefficients in the labor demand equation possess the correct expected signs, and with the exception of the value added per worker, they are all statistically significant at the 1 percent level. The equation shows that the elasticity of employment with respect to TFP is inelastic, suggesting that a 1 percentage increase in TFP would lead to a 0.41 percentage increase in employment. This result is in line with the a priori expectation because the production function that gives rise to the TFP exhibits a decreasing returns to scale. This calls for concerted efforts by the Nigerian authorities to improve the investment climate, thereby enhancing the TFP with its employment-creation capabilities. Thus, there is some evidence that improving firm performance can have a positive effect on employment in the country.

Appendix Table 4   Estimated Conditional Labor Demand

	Estimated coefficient	t-statistic
Log (output per worker)	0.027	0.23
Log (TFP)	0.406***	4.24
Log (wage rate)	−0.789***	6.88
Log (rental cost of capital)	0.158***	4.41
Constant	5.823***	7.56
No. of observations	145	
Adj. R^2	0.604	

Note: t-statistics are in absolute values; *** Significant at the 1 percent level; wage rate is equal to wages per worker, and rental cost of capital is derived from the cost optimization procedure in the production process in which the optimal ratio of capital to labor is proportional to their relative prices.[7]

Notes

1. Weights were not used in any regression analysis.

2. Note that the sample was not stratified by size because such data was not available. The appendix in the full ICA report includes a detailed description of the sampling methodology followed.

3. See for example Subramanian, Anderson, and Lee (2005).

4. For a succinct review of the meanings and methodological approaches to TFP, see Lipsey and Carlaw (2001).

5. The null hypothesis in the Ramsey RESET is that "the model has no omitted variables." The calculated F-ratio from the test is 0.28 with a probability value of 0.85, suggesting that the null hypothesis cannot be rejected, implying that the estimated equation does not suffer from omitted variable bias.

6. The block F-test involves testing a null hypothesis that the difference between all parameters on state dummies is zero. A two-step estimation procedure is carried out with and without the state dummies. The model without the state dummies is the "restricted" model, and that which includes the state dummies is the "unrestricted" model. The difference between the two R-squared values, normalized by the number of state dummies, is then divided by one minus the R-squared from the unrestricted model normalized by the degrees of freedom $(n$-k-$1)$, where n is the number of observations and k is the number of explanatory variables in the unrestricted model. This gives a value for the calculated F that can be compared with the critical value of the F-statistic. In our case, the null hypothesis can be rejected because the probability that $F > 2.1$ is 0.038, suggesting that the coefficients are statistically different at the 5 percent level.

7. This condition can be stated as follows: $(K/L) = \alpha/\beta \, (w/r)$, where α and β are the labor and capital shares in output, respectively (i.e., returns to scale components), and w and r denote wage rate and rental cost of capital, respectively.

Constructing a Composite Investment Climate Index

Methodology

When making an investment decision, entrepreneurs look at a host of factors. These range from cost of inputs, to reliability of infrastructure, to quality of institutions. A sound investment climate indicator should take into account as many of these factors as possible. The investment climate index (ICI) has been built on 44 investment climate variables. The data used were collected in the Enterprise Survey conducted in 11 states in Nigeria in 2007.

For simplicity, the variables are grouped in three categories: inputs, infrastructure, and institutions (Appendix table 5). Within each category two dimensions are identified: objective values (cost) and subjective indicators (perception). As a result of this classification, the 44 variables were grouped in six sets (subindices) that represent the backbone of the ICI and that aim at measuring the cost and quality of infrastructure services, of input markets, and of institutions. Overall, of the 44 variables used, 28 are cost and 16 are perception based. The ICI was then constructed as the weighted index of all subindices. Principal component analysis was used to aggregate the variables because this methodology allows us to identify which variables vary most and hence are more important in determining the quality of the investment climate across Nigerian states.[1]

Appendix Table 5   Variables Used in Construction of Composite Investment Climate

Index (ICI)	
Cost	*Perception*

Infrastructure

1. Size of inventory (transport quality)	1. Electricity constraint
2. Power outages: hrs per shift	2. Transport constraint
3. Water outages: hrs per shift	3. Access to land constraint
4. Power outages: losses (% sales)	
5. Own generator (share of firms)	
6. Electricity from own generator (%)	
7. Own tranportation (share of firms)	
8. Use of own transportation (% of sales)	

Inputs

1. Sales sold on credit (%)	1. Access to finance constraint
2. Sales as intermediate products (%)	2. Cost of finance constraint: Short term
3. Inputs paid before delivery (%)	3. Inadequately educated workforce constraint
4. Improved production processes (share of firms)	
5. Workforce absenteeism: HIV/AIDS	
6. Intereste rate on short-term finance	
7. Share of long-term financing (equity)	
8. Share of firms with loan	
9. Share of firms that need a loan but do not apply	
10. Workforce absenteeism: Malaria	

Institutions

1. Degree of competition	1. Customs constraint
2. Losses due to theft (% sales)	2. Crime constraint
3. Bribes for government contract (% value)	3. Corruption constraint
4. Electric connection days	4. Licensing & permits constraint
5. Degree of gifts requested: Construction	5. Tax rates constraint
6. Visits by tax officials	6. Tax administration constraint
7. Tax evasion (% sales)	7. Functioning of courts constraint
8. Customers' purchase orders in writing	8. Political environment constraint
9. Cost of state regulations	9. Labor regulations constraint
10. Cost of federal regulations	10. Practise of informal sector constraint

Index Reliability

Because there is no theoretical model on the estimation of the weights used in the construction of the index, the reliability of the ICI as a predictor of a good investment climate should be tested by correlating the ICI to indicators of state-level economic performance. Unfortunately there are no available data at the state level in Nigeria for indicators such as domestic private investment, GDP growth, FDI, and per capita income growth. Nevertheless in similar studies in 16 Indian states and in 24 ECA countries, the ICI showed a clear and significant association with all these indicators.[2]

The only state-level indicator available in Nigeria is the Doing Business indicator. A correlation between the ICI and the DB indicator (Appendix figure 1) shows a significant association between the quality of the regulatory environment and the quality of the overall investment climate in our states.[3]

An additional test of reliability was conducted by comparing the state ranking of the ICI with the ranking derived from the perceptions of the managers interviewed during the Enterprise Survey in Nigeria. All the managers were also asked to rank the best and worst states in Nigeria according to what they perceived their business environment to be. Appendix figure 2 presents the ranking of the 11 states according to the responses to this question, and Appendix figure 3 presents how the managers'

Appendix Figure 1   Doing Business Ranking and ICI Ranking in 11 Nigerian States

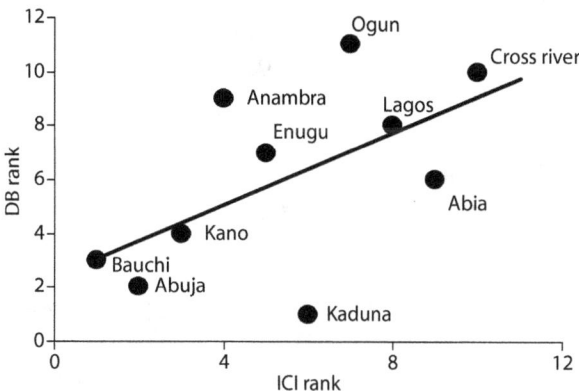

Appendix Figure 2   Managers' Perception of State Ranking of Business Climate

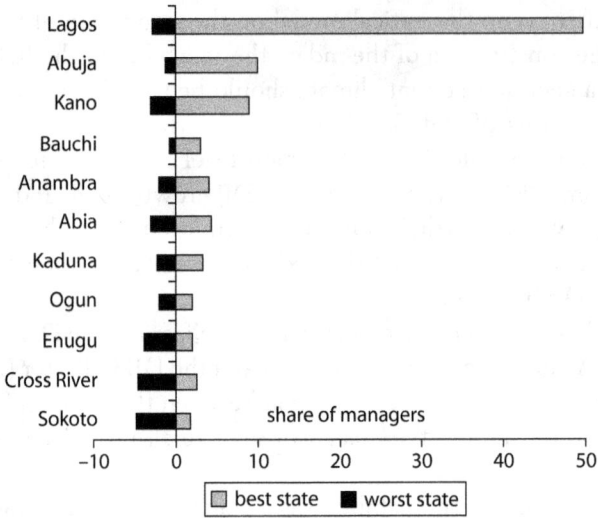

Appendix Figure 3   Managers' Ranking of Worst States and ICI

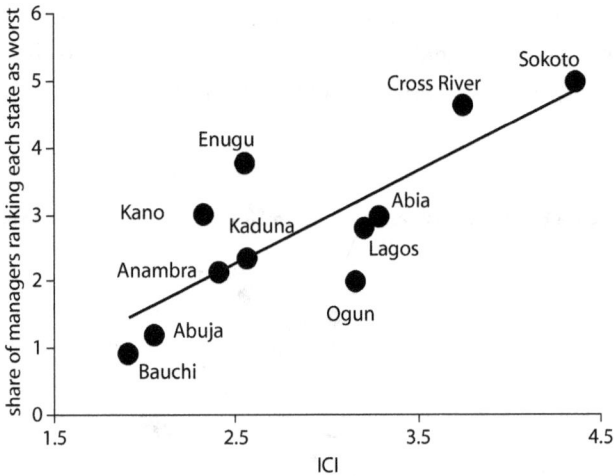

ranking correlates to the ICI ranking for our 11 states. Again the data show a significant association between the ICI and managers' state-level rankings.[4] These tests—along with earlier evidence—provide a certain degree of confidence that the composite ICI is a reliable indicator of the investment climate in Nigeria.

Notes

1. See the full study for a more detailed and technical presentation of the methodology used.

2. The relation between the ICI and private state-level investment in 16 Indian states has been shown to be significant at the 12 percent or 6 percent significance level, depending on the number of outliers excluded. In earlier work in a set of 24 ECA countries, this relationship was shown to be significant (see Iarossi et al. 2007. "Business Climate, Productivity and Competitiveness in Armenia: 2002-2005." *Armenian Journal of Public Policy* 2 (2): 153-91).

3. Sokoto is excluded because it is an outlier, that is, the correlation does not hold for Sokoto.

4. The only outlier is Lagos, perceived by Nigerian managers as the best state.

Index

Figures, notes, and tables are indicated by f, n, and t, respectively.

www.ingramcontent.com/pod-product-compliance
Lightning Source LLC
Chambersburg PA
CBHW070924270326
41927CB00011B/2713